# SOUTH
# RIVIERA
*in your pocket*

Travel Publications

MAIN CONTRIBUTOR: MEG JUMP

PHOTOGRAPH CREDITS
**The Travel Library** title page, back cover, 13, 15, 23, 24, 25 (left, right), 29, 30, 46, 59, 60, 62, 63, 64, 65, 66, 71, 72, 77, 78, 79 (top, bottom), 80, 81, 82, 83, 84, 85, 88, 89 (left), 91 (left, right), 93, 97, 100, 103, 104, 107, 111, 119; The Travel Library/A Amsel 40, 42, 44 (bottom); The Travel Library/Philip Enticknap front cover, 5, 7, 8, 20, 21, 22, 26, 27, 28, 33, 34, 35, 36, 37, 49, 50, 51, 75, 99, 101, 102, 108, 114; The Travel Library/Luke Kelly 19; The Travel Library/ R Richardson 38, 54; Bridgeman Art Library 17, 43; British Film Institute 61; Bob Gibbons 9, 44 (top), 53, 68, 69, 87, 89 (right); Nature Photographers/ Trevor Hall 55.

*Front cover: Hotel Negresco, Nice; back cover: coastal view on the Corniche d'Esterel; title page: Towngate Bridge and River Entrevaux*

MANUFACTURE FRANÇAISE DES PNEUMATIQUES MICHELIN

Place des Carmes-Déchaux – 63000 Clermont-Ferrand (France)

© Michelin et Cie. Propriétaires-Éditeurs 1996

Dépôt légal Avril 96 – ISBN 2-06-630301-1 – ISSN 1272-1689

No part of this publication may be reproduced in any form

without the prior permission of the publisher.

Printed in Spain 3-00/4

**MICHELIN TYRE PLC**
Travel Publications
The Edward Hyde Building
38 Clarendon Road
WATFORD Herts WD1 1SX - UK
☎ (01923) 415000

**MICHELIN TRAVEL PUBLICATIONS**
Editorial Department
One Parkway South
GREENVILLE, SC 29615
☎ 1-800 423-0485

# CONTENTS

# INTRODUCTION

The South of France has been one of the world's most glamorous holiday destinations for almost 200 years. In its heyday it reached the zenith of luxury, a playground for the *crème de la crème* of high society, kings, queens, the super-rich and famous.

Times change and today the Riviera is no longer purely a private enclave of the privileged few, but it still has a wickedly seductive appeal. The ingredients are cloudless skies, brilliant blue seas, olive and orange groves, unspoilt coves and inlets, pine forests, cyprus trees, lavender, bougainvillaea, mimosas, cacti and vines. To all this can be added hill-top medieval villages, picturesque fishing ports, Roman ruins, extravagant Baroque churches, isolated ancient chapels and busy market towns. In addition, if the climate, scenery and architecture are not enough, there are pavement cafés, quayside restaurants, market days, watersports, *boules* matches, fairs and festivals, and art galleries that are amongst the best in the world.

However, there is more to the region than one vast holiday resort. Marseilles, Toulon and Nice are major cities in their own right, and despite the sometimes chaotic development on the coast, just a few kilometres inland much of the region is still basically rural with great areas virtually untouched.

The Riviera that captivated some of our most inspirational writers and painters – a magical combination of azure skies and aquamarine seas – exists today for everyone to see. It is true you will not find many deserted beaches, but splendid isolation never was the Riviera scene.

*Watch the world go by at one of the many outdoor cafés.*

# HOW TO USE THIS GUIDE

This guide is divided into four main sections:

**Background** sets the scene, with an introduction to the geography and landscape of the South of France, an outline of its rich history and development, the legends and heroes, and the culture and people of the South of France today.

**Exploring the South of France** starts with a list of the top sights which should be on everyone's holiday check list. The area is then divided into several regions. Within each is provided a tour of the best and most interesting towns and villages, beaches, landmarks, sights and attractions, providing plenty of ideas for excursions and sight-seeing. Several special sections highlight the best beaches, places to visit inland and sites of specific interest to families.

**Enjoying Your Visit** provides friendly, no-nonsense advice on day-to-day holiday activities which can make the difference between a good holiday and a great one – eating out, shopping, entertainment and nightlife, as well as information about local festivals and the all-important factor, weather.

**A-Z Factfinder** is an easy-to-use reference section packed with useful information, covering everything you may need to know on your visit, from tipping to hiring cars, from using the telephone to vaccinations. A word of warning: opening hours and telephone numbers frequently change, so be sure to check with a local tourist office when planning your visit.

*Yachts moored at the harbour in Cannes.*

## GEOGRAPHY

In modern bureaucratic terms, the official region of Provence-Alpes-Côte d'Azur includes five *départements* (counties): Alpes Maritimes (Nice), Alpes-de-Haute-Provence (Digne), Bouches-du-Rhône (Marseilles), Var (Toulon), Vaucluse (Avignon). In historic and geographical terms, it reaches from the River Rhône in the west to the Italian border in the east; and from a line extending roughly from Orange through Digne in the north, to the Mediterranean coast in the south.

The Riviera coastline is one of tantalizing contrasts. To the east, the massive façade of

*One of the many beautiful beaches along the Côte d'Azur.*

*Stunning scenery on Port-Cros Island (right).*

the maritime Alps that drops dramatically down to the sea protects the coastal communities, endowing them with a beguiling climate in which exotic sub-tropical plants flourish. To the west, the only vegetation able to survive on the arid *calanques* – spectacular fjord-like inlets – is sparse shrubs and stunted trees that cling to the pristine white limestone cliffs. Along the picturesque pine-clad Esterel coast, a mass of startling russet-red porphyric boulders tumble chaotically into the Mediterranean, forming hidden bays and secret coves. Around St-Tropez sweeping expanses of fine sandy beaches are backed by fields of vines.

Inland, the visual contrasts are just as marked. Alpine forests coat the mountainous Nice hinterland; a blanket of Umbrella Pines covers the hills behind Fréjus; and tangled woods of Cork Oak and Sweet Chestnut trees grow on the Massifs des Maures.

Access to the rugged interior was, until recently, relatively difficult. Much of the area was also quite poor in agricultural and other economic resources, resulting in a concentration of population on the coast. Rural towns and villages therefore escaped the rapid development of the coast and have, for the most part, remained delightfully forgotten, authentic and unspoilt. Recently, roads have greatly improved, putting this unexploited hinterland within easy reach, giving holiday-makers on the coast the best of both worlds.

## HISTORY

Since earliest times, humans have been irresistibly attracted to the South of France. Remains in prehistoric caves at Monaco suggest that nomadic tribes had primitive bases there as long ago as 1 000 000 BC. Artifacts discovered around Nice are evidence of permanent settlements from around 400 000 BC onwards; Neanderthal hunters were operating on the Riviera by 60 000 BC; and modern man was active around Marseilles, decorating marine caves at Grotte Cosquer in 30 000 BC.

By 1 000 BC most of the coastal area was loosely under the control of the unruly Ligurians from the east and the zealous Celts from the north until, in 600 BC, the Greeks arrived bringing a new concept of civilization. They set up marine trading stations at Nikaïa (Nice), Antipolis (Antibes) and Massilia (Marseilles), and further changed the landscape of southern France by introducing the olive tree and grape vine.

### Greece and Rome

By the end of the 2C AD the Greeks were forced to request Roman aid in quelling unrest at Nice and Antibes, thus opening the way for Roman domination. Major centres were founded at Cimiez above the Greek port of Nikaïa and at Fréjus – the port constructed to rival Marseilles. In addition to their commercial exploitation of the region, the Romans were the first to use the South of France as a place of recreation and comfortable retirement.

With the fall of Rome in the 5C AD, however, the established order quickly collapsed. Charlemagne brought the Dark Ages to a close, managing to unite much of present-day France but, on his death in 814, his lands were divided between his heirs. In 855 Provence became a separate kingdom ruled over by Charlemagne's grandson, Charles the Bald.

### The Moors and Christians

Soon the Kingdom of Provence became the target of attacks by Saracens from North Africa. Towns were sacked, forcing the local inhabitants to flee to the rugged interior, building mountain-top villages for security. The Saracens too had their own inland stronghold at La Garde-Freinet in the hills behind St-Tropez. It was here in 973 that they were finally defeated by Guillaume le Libérateur.

Christianity had come to southern France during the Roman occupation and from the 11C Provence had independent status within the Holy Roman Empire.

### Italian Influence

Relative peace and stability during the 12C and 13C allowed Provence to prosper and retain its political and cultural independence in western Europe, but there were already signs of division and cultural differences within. From 1186 the power base of the Counts of Provence was Aix but the major towns in the east – especially Nice and Grasse – traditionally had strong links with Genoa and Pisa. Although Provence had witnessed days of unprecedented glory, its days of total independence were numbered, and Provence passed to Louis XI, King of France, in 1481.

In 1388, Nice had been separated from Provence under the terms of a treaty with the House of Savoy, whereby it came under

Italian influence. Although the county of Nice occasionally reverted to France, generally it remained annexed until 1860 when it was finally returned to France.

For centuries, however, the relationship between the County of Nice and France, and especially next-door Provence, was strained, wavering between an uneasy peace and outright war. From 1524 to 1544 there was intense rivalry between François I of France and the Holy Roman Emperor, Charles V, who supported the House of Savoy. Fighting broke out again from 1691 to 1697, causing Louis XIV of France to commission his brilliant military architect, Vauban, to construct extensive fortifications all along the Provence side of the frontier with Savoy, and to fortify the ports of Antibes and Toulon.

### French Revolution

By the second half of the 18C, stricter centralized government from the capital plus increased taxes resulted in social unrest all over France, culminating in 1789 with the Storming of the Bastille in Paris and the terrors of the French Revolution. Nice proved to be a popular haven for aristocratic fugitives and became a centre for anti-revolutionary propaganda during the 'Terror'. In 1793 it was again briefly annexed to France until 1814.

So it was that Napoleon Bonaparte launched his Italian campaign from Nice in 1796. His Egyptian campaign started from Toulon in 1798, returning victoriously to St-Raphaël the following year; and in 1814 the same coastal town was his point of departure for exile on the Mediterranean island of Elba. A year later, he was back in southern

*Luxury yachts in the harbour at St-Tropez.*

France, landing at Golfe-Juan near Antibes, for the long march to Paris.

In 1860 the County of Nice finally came back within French territory as part of a deal in which Napoleon III gave military assistance to the House of Savoy in their fight to drive the Austrians out of northern Italy. In a referendum, the Niçois had voted overwhelmingly to rejoin France.

### Development of the Riviera
The second half of the 19C brought profound changes to the South of France with the advent of tourism and the development of the French Riviera, also known as

the Côte d'Azur (the Azure Coast). From the mid-18C a steady trickle of northern Europeans were visiting Nice, attracted by the mild winters and healthy climate, considered to be particularly kind to consumptives. During the 1820s English residents in Nice contributed towards the widening of a narrow coastal road, the Promenade des Anglais, and in 1834 Lord Brougham discovered Cannes – an unknown fishing village – when his route to Nice was barred due to an epidemic.

By the end of the century the French Riviera was Europe's most fashionable holiday haunt and a choice of elegant resorts – Nice, Cannes, Beaulieu, Monte-Carlo, Menton and Hyères – all built in the contemporary neo-baroque *belle époque* style, were catering for an ever-growing clientele during the mild winter months. Queen Victoria, the Prince of Wales, King Léopold of Belgium, the Russian Tsar and the Aga Khan all had their favourite winter season holiday homes. Artists, writers, musicians and socialites rubbed shoulders with royalty and every night was party night … a dizzy round of distractions for *le beau monde*.

Although southern France was barely touched by World War I its habitual guests most certainly were. After 1918 a different social order evolved within Europe, and the south of France – as charismatic as ever – welcomed a broader spectrum of well-heeled travellers. The Americans – familiar with hot weather – arrived, bringing with them the vogue for sunbathing and sea sports. They launched their own favourite resort at Juan-les-Pins. Between the wars a new generation of liberated fun-seekers made the summer season all the rage and

the Riviera became more relaxed, more cosmopolitan but scarcely less exclusive.

All festivities stopped abruptly with the outbreak of World War II. Italy occupied Menton in 1940 and the French scuttled their own fleet in Toulon harbour before the arrival of the Germans in 1942. The French Resistance was active in the Riviera hinterland – called 'maquis' after the concealing underbrush – until on 14 August, 1944 the Allies began their bombardment of the south coast. The Americans landed at St-Raphaël on the 15th, coordinating with the Free French troops who arrived at St-Tropez the following day. Both towns were severely damaged in the ensuing battle. Hyères, Toulon and Marseilles also came under attack, but by 30 August the Riviera had been liberated.

*Coastal view on the Corniche de l'Esterel between St-Raphaël and Cannes.*

# Painters on the Riviera

Having found inspiration from the luminescence and colourful landscape of inland Provence, painters gravitated to the coast at the end of the last century. Today the major museums in the region contain some of the finest collections of paintings by artists working on the Riviera from the 1890s onwards.

Founder of the Riviera set was the pointillist **Paul Signac** (1863-1935) who discovered the unknown fishing port of St-Tropez in 1892. He built a house here – La Hune – which acted as a catalyst for other painters. Matisse, Bonnard and Dufy were all captivated by the town and became the core of an established Bohemian group. After World War I, St-Paul-de-Vence became a favoured base.

**Auguste Renoir** (1841-1919) was one of the first painters to settle on the Riviera. He came in the 1890s hoping the climate would be beneficial for his rheumatism and bought Les Collettes in Cagnes-Ville in 1906, where he remained for the rest of his life. His studio and home are now open to the public.

**Henri Matisse** (1869-1954), in common with so many painters brought up in the grey north, was first seduced by the vibrant landscape when he visited St-Tropez in 1904. A regular visitor to Nice from 1916, he bought an apartment in the Old Town in 1921 but later moved to Cimiez where he lived and worked until his death. A museum here shows some of his works (*see* p.28). **Pierre Bonnard** (1867-1947) spent his last years at Le Cannet outside Cannes. **Pablo Picasso** (1881-1973) visited Juan-les-Pins in 1921, moving to Vallauris in 1946, and spent most of his later life in the area until he died at Mougins at the age of 92.

**Jean Cocteau** (1889-1963), dramatist and film-maker as well as artist, was a great enthusiast for life on the Riviera. He decorated various chapels and public buildings in the area and personally supervised the creation of a museum for his own paintings at Menton, but died before its opening in 1967.

**Raoul Dufy** (1877-1953)

painted scenes all along the coast from Marseilles to Menton. His works appear in several galleries, as well as the Galerie Raoul Dufy on Cours Saleya in Old Nice.

**Fernand Léger** (1881-1955) lived and worked at Biot, where his dramatic industrial-theme paintings are displayed on the site of his original studio. **Marc Chagall** (1889-1985), who was born in Russia, became a French citizen in 1937 and from 1947 spent most of his time on the Riviera. A major collection of his giant canvases are displayed at Cimiez and he is buried in the cemetery at St-Paul-de-Vence. Another Russian, **Nicolas de Staël** (1914-1955), lived and died at Antibes. His bold, semi-abstract works are exhibited in galleries along the coast.

*The Farmhouse at Cagnes by Auguste Renoir.*

## PEOPLE AND CULTURE

The people of southern France are typically Provençal, and in many ways have more in common with their Mediterranean neighbours – the Italians and Spaniards – than their compatriots from the cooler north. Voluble, expressive and often gregarious, they have an easy-going attitude to life, but can also be volatile and quick-tempered.

### The Language

The traditional language is the *Provençal* version of *langue d'oc* or *occitan*. This is the language that the singing troubadours carried all over southern France during the 14C heyday of Provence. In 1539 it was decreed that French should be the standard language for all administrative processes across the country but the various dialects continued to be spoken, especially in country areas. Even though Provençal enjoyed a revival in the early 20C, the outsider is unlikely to hear it spoken very often in everyday life. However, there is a rich heritage of Provençal poetry and literature; it is taught in schools as an optional subject; and place and street names are often labelled in Provençal as well as French.

Because the County of Nice was separated from Provence between 1388 and 1860, a different language evolved here called *Niçois* or *Nissard* – which you can still hear in the old town of Nice and the remote villages inland. As an independent state, the Principality of Monaco – which originally covered a far larger area than the present day mini-state – also bred its own derivative.

The French spoken all along the coast is quite distinctive, and the Provençaux quickly

*A game of boules in a park in Cannes.*

become very animated; they gesticulate freely, with much shrugging of the shoulders and waving of hands.

### Regional Traditions

In recent years there has been renewed interest in regional traditions and folklore. To see a charmingly authentic aspect of Riviera culture, visit one of the summer village festivals and fairs which often feature lightfooted dancers and strolling pipe and drum musicians. Women wear colourful ankle-length skirts in Provençal fabrics, wide straw bonnets and lacy shawls; men are handsomely dressed in black trousers, white shirts, cummerbunds, waistcoats and rakish black floppy hats. Stalls sell local specialities and craftsmen peddle their wares.

# EXPLORING THE RIVIERA

## MUST SEE

## DAYS OUT

### Nice★★★

Nice is a beautiful city – '*Nissa la Bella*', in the local dialect. Superbly sited on the sweeping curve of the **Baie des Anges** and set against a dramatic backdrop of Alpine foothills, for much of the year Nice is bathed

*Cloudless skies over the Old Town district of Nice.*

in luminous Mediterranean sunshine, colourful with exotic flowers and sub-tropical plants. As the unofficial, but generally accepted, capital of the French Riviera, it is a vibrant and progressive university city that has been in the hospitality business for over 200 years. With a population of 475 000, it is the fifth largest city in France and has the second busiest airport, making it the most important entry point to the South of France for overseas visitors. There is, however, far more to Nice than simply mass tourism. Politically divided from the rest of France for 500 years from 1388 to 1860, the Niçois people, their food, architecture and language have a marked individual flavour and cultural identity.

First impressions are important and most people arrive in the city via the **Promenade des Anglais★★** – one of the world's most

*The Baie des Anges sweeps past Nice.*

*The Promenade des Anglais with the Hotel Negresco in the background, Nice.*

famous seaside boulevards. Stroll along its 4km (2.5 miles) length, and get deliciously lost in the tropical foliage of the **Parc Phoenix★** (Phoenix Park), with the impressive **Musée des Art Asiatiques★★** (Museum of Asian Arts) built on the lake by the Japanese architect, Kenzo Tange. Around the corner from the Law Faculty, Fragonard, Van Loo, Dufy, Van Dongen and the enigmatic *niçois* Symbolist, Mossa, await you at the **Musée des Beaux-Arts Jules Chéret★** (Jules Chéret Museum of Fine Arts) in a beautiful neo-Renaissance villa. Or you might prefer the originality of Croatian artists such as Generalic or Rabuzin, exhibited at the **Musée d'Art Naïf A. Jakovsky★** (A. Jakovsky Museum of Naive Art). On Boulevard Gambetta, the gilded onion domes of the **Cathédrale Orthodoxe St-Nicolas★** (St Nicolas Orthodox Cathedral) are a reminder that the Russian aristocracy appreciated the Côte d'Azur sun. But, above all, this long promenade lapped by the sea, shaded by palm trees, lined with modern buildings – some of Italiante architecture like that which houses the **Musée Masséna★** (Massena Museum), standing beside flamboyant *belle époque* hotels such as the famous **Negresco** – will provide an excellent insight into the splendours of the Riviera of yesteryear.

*Parc Phoenix in Nice.*

The promenade leads to the city centre via the Albert I Gardens, which open onto **Place Masséna**, surrounded by arcaded buildings with red-rendered façades, a strategic spot from which, at Mardi Gras, to join in the celebrations during the famous **Carnaval de Nice★★** (Nice Carnival). The shopping streets begin from here: **Avenue Jean Médecin** with its department stores, and the pedestrianised **Rue Masséna**, with its small restaurants and designer boutiques.

*Rue de la Préfecture in Old Nice.*

Modern art lovers won't want to miss the **Museum of Contemporary Art**★★ where, among the masters of the *avant garde*, they'll encounter the dynamic **École de Nice** (Nice School) (Yves Klein, Ben, etc). Not far from there the **Acropolis-palais des Congrès**★ (Acropolis Convention Center), with its sculptures by Arman and César, complete this panorama of contemporary arts.

**Old Nice**★ The great thing about the **old quarter** is that it is very much a living city, not just a historic tourist attraction. The warren of streets in the old town can be confusing and are best explored with the help of a good map. Take the street behind the 18C Triton fountain in Place Masséna, go along Rue St-François-de-Paule, passing by **Alziari's**, famous for home-pressed olive oil, and the **Opera House** offering a programme of concerts and ballet as well as opera throughout the year, to the picturesque central square, **Cours Saleya**. This has a perfumed flower market daily except on Monday, when an antiques market takes over. Soak up the atmosphere at one of the pavement cafés, over a leisurely seafood meal.

*One of the pavement cafés in Old Town Nice (left).*

*A display of the famed olive oil of the region (right).*

*Many of the harbours in the south of France are still active fishing ports, and seafood on the menu is a speciality of the region.*

From Cours Saleya a labyrinth of streets fan out, lined by tall Italianate houses and a number of splendid 17C churches, prettily painted outside and an exubcrant riot of colour and candles within. Look out especially for the **Cathédrale Ste-Réparate**, with its superb dome of glazed tiles and its sumptuous Baroque **décor★**; the Église St-Jacques (or Gesù), decorated with painted sculpted cherubs; and, above all, the **Chapelle de la Miséricorde★** (Misericord Chapel) built by the Black Penitents in 1740, featuring a fine Rococo interior and, in the sacristy, two altar-pieces by *niçois* primitive artists Jean Miralhet and Louis Bréa.

However, the architectural highlight of Old Nice is the 17C **Palais Lascaris** in Rue Droite, a fabulous palace originally belonging to the aristocratic Lascaris family from Ventimiglia. Quite small by palatial standards and with a rather ordinary exterior, inside it is a veritable treasure trove of extravagant Baroque décor and traditional *trompe l'œil* ceiling frescoes.

Old Nice has much more than historic houses. A plethora of fascinating shops (many close on Mondays) offer fascinating browsing. Look out for **pasta shops** and for displays of delicious ready-cooked take-away food. To see the variety of locally caught Mediterranean fish, head for the **fish market** at Place St-François (daily except Monday).

For a hassle-free mini-tour of Old Nice, take *le petit train* – the white tourist tram-

*The waterfall at the Château in Nice.*

train that leaves the Promenade des Anglais opposite the Méridien Hotel. It winds its way through the pedestrian streets of the old town before climbing up to the **Château**. Constructed in the 10C, fortified by the Counts of Provence and later occupied by the Dukes of Savoy, the castle was totally destroyed in 1706, but the hill retains the name. The panoramic **views★★** over Nice and the Baie des Anges are superb. Return on the little train, or walk down through the pleasant **château gardens**, or descend via the lift that arrives at a point on the coast road just before the port. Constructed in the 18C, the **harbour** is small with relatively shallow waters. It is an excellent place to sample the *niçois* version of the fish soup *bouillabaisse* and is the main embarkation quay for ferries to Corsica.

**Cimiez★★** The hill-top residential suburb of Cimiez is another 'must' and is easy to reach

on the number 15 bus. Developed first by the Romans, and later favoured by the English aristocracy, it is noted today for the **Roman remains★** of a small arena and well-preserved thermal bath complex, dating from the 3C AD. This is the atmospheric venue for open-air concerts during the Jazz Festival (Jazz à Nice) in July.

The **Musée Matisse★★** (Matisse Museum) is housed in the 17C Genoese-style **Villa des Arènes**. This uses multimedia examples of Matisse's work to give an insight into the life

*A view over Bassin Lympia in Nice.*

of the artist, who spent the last decades of his life at Cimiez. The **Musée Marc-Chagall★★** (Marc-Chagall Museum) includes 17 large, brightly coloured canvases, plus hundreds of studies from 1954-1967 depicting Old Testament scenes.

## Nice to Menton

Between Nice and the Italian border overland travel has always been difficult due to the stark mountains that rise immediately behind the coast. Today, in addition to the highly functional but unlovely **autoroute** that carves a direct line from behind Nice all the way to Genoa, with feeder roads down

*Musée Marc Chagall – where colour, dreams and fantasy unite to deliver Chagall's message.*

*The autoroute behind Menton cuts its way through the idyllic scenery of the Riviera.*

to the seaside resorts, three roads traverse the rugged, and often breathtakingly beautiful, terrain.

**The Grande Corniche★★★** This is the most exciting route, following the ancient Roman **Aurelian Way**. Bleak and desolate in places, the road reaches a height of 450m (1 476ft) and offers wonderful views over the Riviera coastline to the south, and to the distant Alps in the north. Some stretches are well inland, and of the few villages it passes, one

*Looking down to Monaco from La Turbie.*

of the most interesting is **La Turbie★**, with its great triumphal monument (Trophée des Alpes). This was erected in 6 BC to celebrate Rome's victory over the last remaining local tribes. The village retains two medieval gateways, houses dating back to the 11C, and an 18C church (constructed with stone plundered from the Roman monument) with fine religious paintings, two by **Van Loo**, one attributed to **Veronese**.

Further along the Grande Corniche, as it descends to the sea, it is worth stopping off at **Roquebrune★**. Clinging to the side of a hill, the perched village takes its name from the russet-coloured façades of the ancient houses that cluster around a sturdy 10C fortress, built to fight off marauding Saracens. Just outside the village, towards Menton, look out for the olive tree reputed to be over 1 000 years old.

**The Middle Corniche★★** The Middle Corniche is the most popular and pictur-esque of the coastal roads (and therefore often uncomfortably congested). Dramatic-ally poised on a cliff 427m (1 401ft) above the sea, the medieval hill village of **Èze★★**, with its ruined 14C castle, seems to be suspended in mid-air. Views from here are stunning and, on a clear day, Corsica is often visible. Èze is now one of the most visited and fashionable attractions on the Riviera, with prestigious hotels and restaurants lining its carefully preserved, traffic-free streets.

**The Lower Corniche★★** This runs at sea level, giving access to all the coastal resorts. It is always busy, so a sensible alternative is to use the excellent train service that follows more or less the same route. First stop round the coast is the pretty fishing port of **Ville-franche**★ on one of the deepest and most enclosed natural bays of the Riviera. It is guarded by a formidable 16C citadel and sturdy fortifications, occupied today by the **Musée Volti**★, dedicated to this local rival of Maillol. The unspoilt **old town**★ climbs steeply from the lively waterfront with gaily painted houses, restaurants and pavement cafés. Look for the vaulted medieval **Rue Obscure** and the 14C **Chapelle St-Pierre**★ (Chapel of St Pierre), lavishly decorated by Jean Cocteau in 1957. An antique market is held at Villefranche every Sunday.

To drive round the ultra-exclusive and idyllic **Cap Ferrat**★★ peninsula, turn off the Corniche just beyond Villefranche, and discover how the seriously rich live on the Riviera. King Léopold II of Belgium began the trend last century when he built his holiday home, Les Cèdres. In 1906 he added Villa Mauresque, later bought by Somerset Maugham. The magnificent villas are invariably surrounded by high hedges and barred gates but part of King Léopold's estate is now a zoo (open daily). The fabulous pastel-pink **Ephrussi-de-Rothschild Foundation**★★ (Villa Ile de France), completed by heiress Baroness Ephrussi de Rothschild in 1912 to house her priceless art collection of paintings, porcelain, tapestries and furniture, is also open to the public, as are the glorious gardens. There are superb **views**★★ from the lighthouse at the tip of the cape. The former fishing village of **St-Jean-Cap-Ferrat**★ has good seafood restaurants.

**Beaulieu**★★, with its palm-fringed promenade, *belle époque* architecture, grand hotels, formal gardens and a casino, is one of the typical old-style Riviera resorts. The

*Sumptuous jewel of the Ephrussi-de-Rothschild Villa, the gardens hint of ocean voyages past – in a breathtaking setting, a magnificent floral symphony to the background melody of the sea's swell.*

pleasure boat marina with quayside restaurants is a more recent addition. **Villa Kérylos★**, built between 1902-1908 by archaeologist Théodore Reinach, as an authentic reproduction of a classic Greek villa, stands on a fine **site★** overlooking the sea and Cap-Ferrat. Lavish use of Carrera marble, alabaster and exotic woods, copies of frescoes and many original Greek ornaments make this a remarkable museum.

*Sun worshippers on the beach at Beaulieu.*

**Monaco★★★** The tiny Principality of Monaco is best approached from **La Turbie★**. This spectacular drive offers some of the finest views on the Riviera. It was on this road that Princess Grace tragically met her death in 1982.

Tightly packed into less than 2sq km (0.8sq miles), roughly half the size of New York's Central Park, Monaco is the world's second smallest sovereign state, after Vatican City. Crammed between the sea and mountains, expansion has had to be vertical, resulting in an intricate development of high-rise blocks packed side by side on steep terraces, juxtaposed with flamboyant hotels and villas from the *belle époque* era. Lack of income tax has lured the world's wealthy so well that only 20 per cent of the 30 000 population are actually Monégasque.

As an independent state closely tied to France, Monaco is ruled over with determination and tenacity by the **Grimaldis**, who bought control from Genoa in the 14C. Today's jet-setting super-star royal family contribute to the mini-state's universal appeal.

*The Prince's Palace in Monaco.*

*Shops and cafés are scattered all over the old town of Monaco.*

Formerly a 13C fortress, the crenellated **Palais du Prince**★ (Prince's Palace) stands on **Le Rocher**★★ (The Rock). There is no vehicular access, except for buses, to this sheer promontory with lovely **views**★★ out to sea. Traditionally watched over by Monégasque *carabiniers*, the daily changing of the guard ceremony at 11.55am is a popular spectacle, but the palace, with its priceless furniture and frescoes, is only open to the public at certain times during the summer months.

The picturesque narrow streets of the old town – now given over to souvenir shops and cafés – are dominated by the **Cathedral**. Built in the 19C on the site of a 12C church, the interior contains a superb collection of **paintings**★★ by *niçois* primitive artists, including Louis Bréa. The much acclaimed **Musée Océanographique**★★★

*The Cathedral in Monaco.*

(Oceanographic Museum) is one of the principal marine museums in Europe. Founded in 1910, it features over 5 000 species of fish and acts as a research centre which, for many years, was managed by the famous Jacques-Yves Cousteau.

On The Rock, history lovers will enjoy the **Musée Napoléonien et des Archives du Palais★** (Napoleon Museum and Palace Archives). Those who are still children at heart may prefer the **Musée National de Monaco – Musée des Poupées et des**

**Automates★** (Monaco National Museum – Doll and Automaton Museum), whilst others will linger at length in front of the sumptuous collection of **vintage cars★** belonging to the royal family.

The 19C town of **Monte-Carlo★★★** – with the Casino at its heart – is the real attraction in Monaco. To try and boost the state's dwindling finances, the first casino opened in 1862 at a time when gambling was strictly banned in most other European countries, including France. Like a magnet, it drew wealthy gamblers from far and wide, and even when gaming laws were eventually

*The Café de Paris in Monte-Carlo.*

relaxed elsewhere, so exclusive and exciting had Monte-Carlo become that the rich and famous continued to flock there.

To cater to the Casino's patrons, many luxurious establishments were built, including the exclusive **Hôtel de Paris**, the **Hôtel L'Hermitage** with its superb glass winter-garden, designed by Gustave Eiffel, and the **Café de Paris**, an Art Deco gem.

The present magnificent **Casino**, which was opened in 1878, has changed very little. Built in the extravagant *belle époque* style,

*The world-famous casino of Monte-Carlo.*

heavily adorned outside, amazingly opulent within, the gaming rooms are open free to the gambling or the non-gambling public. The adjoining **Salle Garnier** (Opera House) is equally splendid.

**La Condamine**, the harbour area between The Rock and Monte-Carlo, was once a working port, but the quaysides are now mainly moorings for luxury boats, including the Monégasque royal yacht. This is the arrival point for cars in the Monte-Carlo Rally, and the Monaco Grand Prix motor racing circuit passes alongside.

On a cliff high above La Condamine with panoramic **views★**, the **Jardin Exotique★★** (Tropical Gardens) contain a vast collection of rare cacti, grasses and other sub-tropical plants. The mineral rocks of the **Grotte de l'Observatoire★** (Observatory Cave), which were inhabited 2000 000 years ago, will whet the appetite for a visit to the fascinating **Musée d'Anthropologie Préhistorique★** (Prehistoric Anthropology Museum).

To the west of The Rock, the new town of **Fontvieille** was constructed in the 1980s on reclaimed land. Connected to Monte-Carlo by tunnels under The Rock, it consists of a residential marina development and vast sports complex. Monaco's diverse light industries such as food processing and textiles are also based here. These activities have so successfully balanced the principality's economy, that only five percent of Monaco's revenue now comes directly from gambling.

**Menton★★** Almost on the frontier, Menton is – not surprisingly – the most Italianate of the old French towns. Formerly attached to the powerful independent state of Genoa, Menton remained under the rule of the

*The harbour at Menton.*

Grimaldis of Monaco from 1346 until 1861, when it was attached to France. Set around two natural bays divided by a headland and 17C fort (now the **Musée Jean-Cocteau**), the medieval city remains wonderfully unspoilt, evocative and intact. Steep streets, lined by houses with façades in a myriad of mellow ochre tones, rise from the quayside ramparts to converge at **Parvis St-Michel★★**, the paved square which makes a superb setting for open-air evening concerts in summer. Dominating both the square and the skyline, the splendid 17C Baroque church of **St-Michel** is flanked by two campanile towers, the tallest of which reaches 53m (174ft).

Menton is also reputed for its balmy climate, a haven for the lush vegetation

which thrives here, particularly citrus fruits (a colourful lemon festival is held each February). Don't miss a visit to **Menton's gardens★** – the tropical **Val Rameh★**, created in 1930 by the English, and the **Romanciers**, with its typically Spanish influence, designed by the writer Blasco Ibáñez.

The 17C and 18C town contains many fine buildings. The **Palais Carnolès**, old summer palace of the Grimaldis, now houses the **Musée des Beaux-Arts★** (Museum of Fine Arts), containing works by French and Italian painters from the 13C to 18C plus paintings by Graham Sutherland, who was an honorary citizen of Menton. The **Registry Office** (Salle des Mariages) at the Town Hall was decorated by Jean Cocteau and the **Municipal Museum**, with its Italianante façade, has many fine local archaeological finds, plus paintings by Utrillo and Dufy.

If you happen to be in Menton on a Friday, you will find an **antique market** in the pedestrian shopping area at Place des Herbes, and you may want to pop over the Italian border to the enormous Friday street market at Ventimiglia. Take passports but no Italian currency: French francs are accepted.

## Nice to Cannes

West of Nice the River Var marks the natural frontier between Provence and the old County of Nice. Now densely populated and overshadowed by the unmistakable bulk of Marina Baie des Anges – a massive curved and wedge-shaped apartment block that dominates the skyline for kilometres around – the immediate coastline is over-commercialized. Far better to head inland where, amongst sparse pine forests, hints of former fertile farmland survive: terraced

olive groves, market gardens, pockets of
mimosas and fields of flowers. The historic
hill-top village of **Haut-de-Cagnes**★ is crowned
by **Château Grimaldi**★, another maritime
fortress built by the powerful lords of
Monaco. The castle was transformed into a
splendid palace in the mid-1600s and retains
many of its best Renaissance features: a
galleried courtyard with 200-year-old pepper
tree, the chapel and a fine ceiling painted by
Giovanni Carlone in 1620. It also contains a
**museum**★ dedicated to the olive tree and
various art collections. In the newer town of
**Cagnes-Ville**★, the former home and studio
of Renoir, set amongst his garden and olive
groves, is preserved as it was when he died as
the **Musée Renoir**. At nearby Villeneuve-
Loubet, in the house that was once the family

*The village of Haut-
de-Cagnes, with
Château Grimaldi
at centre stage.*

Les Collettes, *one Renoir's works in the Renoir Museum.*

*Ochres and browns in perfect harmony; squares bathed in the gentle sound of fountain water; steep, narrow side streets criss-crossed with steps – St-Paul-de-Vence echoes the gentle pace of life in Provence.*

home of Escoffier, the **Musée de l'Art Culinaire** (Culinary Museum) documents the life and achievements of France's greatest chef.

**St-Paul-de-Vence★★** Many of the towns and villages dotted amongst the hills are associated with artists and craftsmen. St-Paul-de-Vence, the most picturesque, fashionable and famous, was built on a splendid hill-top position a few kilometres from the sea to avoid Saracen attack. In the 1920s the village was discovered by painters such as Bonnard, Modigliani, Signac and Soutine, and since then it has become local legend how, as struggling artists, they met in the village inn where the proprietor was prepared to accept their better paintings in exchange for food and wine. Eventually the painters gained

*43*

*Flowers adorn a doorway in St-Paul-de-Vence.*

recognition and the inn became **La Colombe d'Or** – a renowned hotel and restaurant with one of the finest private 20C art collections on its walls. (To see the paintings you will have to have a meal.) You can walk around the village's 16C **ramparts★**, which offer fine views over mimosa, olive and orange groves to the sea. Or you could browse amongst the workshops and galleries in the 16C arcades on Rue Grande. Don't forget the gold reliquaries and a painting attributed to Tintoretto in the 12C church. On a more recent note, the **Fondation Maeght★★** (Maeght Foundation), hidden in pine woods outside the village, is acknowledged as one of the world's finest collections of 20C art, and

includes works by Picasso, Matisse, Braque, Chagall, Giacometti, Leger, Miró and Calder.

**Vence★** Though larger and perhaps lesser known, Vence does not lack interest or charm. An ancient bishopric and busy market town with a rich history, it has long attracted artists. (D. H. Lawrence died here in 1930.) Although surrounded by villa developments, the old quarter, encircled by high 15C walls, is well preserved and alive with shops, studios, restaurants and bars. **Place du Frêne** takes its name from a giant ash tree said to have been planted to commemorate visits in the 16C by François I and Pope Paul III; and **Place du Peyra★**, with its splashing fountain, is believed to be built on the forum of the original Roman town. The **Cathedral** stands on the site of a 5C temple to Mars and contains exceptional carved choir stalls from the mid-15C. Tucked away in a residential suburb, the highlight of the town is the movingly simple **Chapelle du Rosaire★** (Chapel Rosaire, also called Chapelle Matisse) that Matisse designed and decorated for Dominican nuns between 1947 and 1951, in gratitude for nursing him through a serious illness.

**Other Towns and Villages** The pretty fortified village of **Tourrettes-sur-Loup★** has always been associated with violets. Traditionally cultivated under olive trees, the flowers are either crystallized or sent to the perfume factories of Grasse. A **Violet Festival** takes place in March and the village is also a centre for numerous craftspeople. **Vallauris** has been a pottery town for centuries but had rather lost momentum until Picasso's arrival in the 1940s, when he revitalized traditional skills. Over 100

*The hill-top town of St-Paul-de-Vence.*

*The picturesque village of Tourrettes-sur-Loup.*

artisans are now working in the town. **Biot★**, a delightful medieval craft town also famous for pottery, produces distinctive hand-blown bubble-flecked glassware and was home to the modern artist, Léger, until his death in 1955. His studio has been extended to house the **Musée Fernand-Léger★★** (Fernand Léger National Museum), a dramatic display of nearly 400 of his works, showing his development from post-Impressionist to post-Cubist, including huge ceramics, vast mosaics, stained glass and tapestries.

**Antibes★★** Antibes is rich in history and packed with interest. It is set beside a deep sheltered bay where the Greeks formed a maritime trading post in 600 BC, calling it Antipolis. Then came the Romans and, centuries later, the French kings recognized

its strategic importance as a stronghold at the end of the Baie des Anges overlooking Nice. The port and headland fortress – **Fort Carré** – were heavily fortified by Vauban in the 17C and in 1794 Bonaparte lodged in the town while supervising coastal defences.

In 1970 the commercial harbour was converted for pleasure craft. With over 1 200 berths, Port Vauban is one of the major pleasure boat ports on the Mediterranean and a base for professional charter yachts and cruisers as well as amateur sailors.

Protected by impressive ramparts on the seaward side, the **old town★** is lively and full of charm. Just within the town walls, the 17C **Cathedral** (built on the site of a 10C church) features a 12C belfry converted from a former watch-tower, a Romanesque apse and a fine 15C wooden crucifix. Built high on a sea-facing terrace, the 12C **Château Grimaldi** houses a museum dedicated to Picasso. The artist worked here in 1946 on some of his major works, which he then gave to the town when he left. Named the **Donation Picasso★** (Picasso Donation), it contains Mediterranean-inspired paintings as well as ceramics created in Vallauris. In his old studio, look out for the works of Nicolas de Staël and, on the terrace, sculptures by Richier, Miró and Spoerri. Close by, don't miss the **Musée Peynet★** (Peynet Museum) dedicated to this artist, famous in France for his *Amoureux*. Below the chateau is the daily covered market on Cours Masséna, and on Thursdays a colourful Provençal market spills into the streets. On the landward side of the old town, the 19C quarter is now a busy pedestrianized shopping precinct.

The scenic peninsula south of Antibes – **Cap d'Antibes★** – is one of the most exclusive enclaves of the Riviera, where millionaires' mansions nestle, well concealed amongst pine woods. Take the road around the cape, stopping off at Pointe Bacon for the best views of Antibes and Fort Carrée, to the **Musée Naval et Napoléonien** (Naval and Napoleonic Museum), commemorating Napoleon's numerous activities on this coast. Also hidden away on this southern tip is the famous ultra-smart Hôtel du Cap described by F. Scott Fitzgerald in *Tender is the Night*. Inland on the **Garoupe Plateau**, the strange little chapel complex of Notre-Dame has panoramic **views★★** towards Antibes. The lighthouse on the same site is one of the most powerful in France with a beam that reaches 70km (43 miles) out to sea. Nearby **Villa Thuret**'s 10ha (25 acres) of **gardens★** are devoted to over 8 000 species of Mediterranean plants and trees, plus a botanical research centre.

On the west coast of Cap d'Antibes lies **Juan-les-Pins★★★**, with one of the best sandy beaches, where pine trees reach down to the water's edge. Newest of the old-style luxury Riviera playgrounds and brainchild of American millionaire Frank Jay Gould, who lured high society stars such as F. Scott Fitzgerald and Ernest Hemingway here in the 1920s and 30s, the resort has always been a favourite with young sophisticates. The hectic nightlife that goes on late centres around the **Casino** in streets full of bars, restaurants and night clubs. In July, the **Jazz Festival** is a major international event attracting the world's best musicians.

**Cannes★★★** Ribbon development along the coast passes through Golfe-Juan, where

Napoleon landed in 1815 after his escape from Elba, and into Cannes – last of the true Riviera resorts. With a population of just under 70 000, Cannes has grown from a small fishing village to a highly successful convention centre and a very up-market holiday town. It is the most blatantly smart and cosmopolitan of resorts but never really had the rich history and cultural heritage of either Nice or Monte-Carlo.

Part of its success in recent decades is due to the fashionable and famous **Film Festival**, held in May. Focused around the massive modern **Festival and Conference Centre** opened in 1982, the occasion attracts the cream of the entertainment world, and a bevy of paparazzi. Everything that happens

*Sun, sea and sand at the beach in Cannes.*

in Cannes happens around **Boulevard de la Croisette★★** – the elegant seaside boulevard bordered by palm trees, gardens and fine sandy beaches – scene of so many starlet photos during the Film Festival. At the eastern end, the legendary **Carlton Hotel** stands in all its 355-bedroomed ornate *belle époque* glory. Built in 1911, the unmistakable white stucco façade is flanked by twin towers capped with shiny black cupolas, said to have been inspired by the breasts of the architect's gypsy mistress. The **Festival Palace** with its conference rooms, casino and walkway, with handprints of visiting celebrities set into the pavement, occupies the central position.

*A view of Cannes harbour.*

In contrast, the old port at the foot of **Le Suquet**, lined with bars, restaurants and shops, overlooks the harbour where common fishing boats are moored beside luxury yachts. Tourist boats leave from the *gare maritime* on trips to the Lérins Islands.

For the best in designer shopping, go to the classy boutiques on **Rue d'Antibes**, but for local specialities and souvenirs, **Rue Meynadier** is best. As evening falls, take in the views from the 12C watch tower high above the old town, or walk out to **Pointe de la Croisette★** and see the sun go down in the west. As cocktail hour approaches, Cannes is the place to stroll around and be seen; take

*The imposing façade of the Hôtel de Ville (town hall), Cannes.*

an aperitif at a pavement café on the Boulevard de la Croisette or one of the bars in the smart hotels. After a leisurely dinner, try your luck at the Casino Croisette or, in summer, at the Palm Beach Casino on Pointe de la Croisette.

No visit to Cannes is complete without a trip to the offshore **Iles de Lérins★★** (Lérins Islands). Only a few kilometres south and clearly visible from land, they are a world away from the bustle of Cannes. Havens of tranquil glades and verdant forests, the two islands were inhabited by the monks of Lérins, one of the most powerful monastic orders in Christendom. The smaller of the islands, **St-Honorat★★**, just 1.5km (1 mile) long and 400m (1 312ft) wide, takes its name from St Honoratus who founded a monastery here in the 4C. The island is still the property of Cistercian monks and is partially cultivated with lavender and vines. But visitors may walk around the island and see the inhospitable **fortified monastery★** built in 1073 by the Abbot of Lérins to keep the Saracens at bay, and the woodland chapels of Trinity, St-Saviour and St-Caprias. The abbey was restored and extended in the 19C but may only be visited by prior arrangement. A small **museum** and the **abbey church** are open to the public. Redesigned by Viollet-le-Duc (who also restored Carcassonne) in the Romanesque style, the church retains an original 11C Chapel of the Dead.

Separated by a narrow strait 1km (0.6 mile) wide, **Ste-Marguerite★★** is twice the size of its twin and only 15 minutes from Cannes. Named after the sister of St Honoratus who founded an order of nuns, the island is a wonderland for walkers.

Densely covered with **forests★★** of fragrant eucalyptus trees and Aleppo Pine, the interior and the entire coastline are interlaced with clearly marked woodland footpaths. The only habitation is **Fort Royal**, built as a castle in the 1620s and converted to a state prison in 1685. Situated on the north coast, there are superb views from the fort back over the sea to Cannes. The main attraction here is the dank dungeon where the mysterious '**man in the iron mask**' was incarcerated from 1687 to 1698 before being moved to the Bastille where he died in 1703. His true identity is still pure speculation. A marine museum on the same site displays artifacts dating back to the Roman period.

*Its clumps of mauve light up the countryside, its perfume almost heady – lavender, soul of haute Provence!*

*A perfume factory in Grasse.*

The **Route Napoléon★★** traces the passage north taken by the exiled emperor after his landing at Golfe-Juan in 1815 and his cold reception by the people of Cannes. Passing through **Mougins** – a fashionable hill-top village which has become something of a mecca for gourmets due to the surprising choice of excellent restaurants – the road leads to the perfume town of **Grasse★★**. Once a tannery centre, the town became involved in perfumery with the 16C vogue for scented gloves. The tanneries have disappeared but scent-making survives and Grasse is the world's major producer of heady essences that are blended to make the most famous perfumes. The three producers in Grasse – Fragonard, Gallimard and Molinot – are all open daily and offer free tours around their factories. The **Musée International de la Parfumerie★** (International Perfume Museum) gives a fascinating insight into the history of the industry. Whilst in Grasse, visit the **Villa-Musée Fragonard** (Fragonard Museum), containing works by Jean-Honore Fragonard (1732-1806) who was born in the town, and the **old town★** where the cathedral has three paintings by Rubens.

## Cannes to St-Tropez

West of Cannes is **La Napoule★** with its smart marina and solid 14C chateau housing a **museum** created by the eccentric American millionaire sculptor Henry Clew. From here the distant mountain silhouette of the Massif de l'Esterel dramatically announces a change in terrain. The picturesque Var coastline with its expanses of superb sandy beaches bordered by pine forests, backed by vine-yards, has a very different atmosphere from the Alpine foothills further east. The dozens of seaside resorts that boomed in the 1960s and 70s catered for a new breed of budget-conscious tourists, for family holidays and a younger set of fun-and-sun-seeking travellers.

**The Esterel\*\*\*** In stark contrast to the endless resorts that stretch to the Italian border and beyond, the wild and desolate **Esterel mountains\*\*\*** come as an unexpected – but welcome – surprise. Composed of contorted masses of highly coloured porphyric volcanic rock in tones of startling russet-red, the densely forested terrain sinks into deep valleys and rises to the highest point of 620m (2 034ft) at **Mont Vinaigre\*\***. Although frequently ravaged by forest fires, certain areas are designated as

*The Esterel hills.*

special reserves under the control of the National Forestry Commission which ensure that the wonderful flora of the Esterel, including mimosa, oleander and flowering cacti, is well able to survive and thrive.

A spectacular **coastal road★★★** (Corniche d'Or) offers breathtaking views at almost every tortuous bend, as a gorgeous tangle of red-rock outcrops tumble haphazardly into an aquamarine sea. On a fine day the rocks appear to shimmer and take on a luminous glow and in early spring the hillsides turn to gold when the mimosa is in bloom. Only a handful of discreet developments disturb this untamed coastline until **Agay★** – a delightful seaside town on a sweeping natural bay with safe sandy beaches. An ideal spot for windsurfers and a favourite with families, there is no frenetic nightlife and no marina but the deep waters of the bay provide excellent moorings for an assortment of craft. Agay is also the centre for exploration inland, either by pony or mountain bike, both of which are available at Domaine du Fenouillet, 3km (1.8 miles) north of Agay on Route de Valescure.

On leaving Agay, the pine-clad hills are dappled with holiday villas and a group of well-established small resorts run one into the other, leading to **St-Raphaël★**. This animated town began life as a holiday retreat for wealthy Romans, but sprang to popularity when the Parisians discovered it at the end of the 19C. A casino and a new busy marina, plus a vast golf complex at **Valescure** give it year-round appeal. Throughout the summer, boats depart from the Old Port for trips around the Esterel coast, to offshore islands and across the bay to **Port-Grimaud★** and St-Tropez.

To traverse the Esterel inland you will
need to negotiate the Esterel Gap – the old
Roman road from Rome to Aix which has
become today's Route Nationale 7. From
Mandelieu outside Cannes, the road slowly
twists and turns through a wilderness of
dramatic forest scenery to the sole
substantial community in the area, **Les
Adrets**. This pleasant village built of typical
reddish Esterel rock, is the main inland
centre for discovering the Esterel, especially
Mont Vinaigre.

**Fréjus★** Fréjus rose to prominence as an
episcopal city during the 11C and the
**Cathedral★** of St-Léonce is still the hub of
the modern town. Seat of the powerful
Bishops of Fréjus, the **massively fortified
cathedral compound★★** is a supreme
example of Romanesque and early Gothic
architecture. Built in attractive mellow stone
and constructed on the site of the original
Roman town, the complex includes a 4C
**baptistery★★** (spared by the Saracens) with
Corinthian columns from a former Roman
pagan temple and double-storey **cloisters★★**
decorated with 14C paintings. The cathedral
has fine 12C vaulting, richly decorated choir
stalls and a superb carved Renaissance
doorway. A collection of antiquities from the
Gallo-Roman period is housed next to the
cloisters and art exhibitions are displayed in
the crypt.

The town is compact and lively, with a
busy market and outdoor craft stalls on
summer evenings. It makes a good centre
for exploring the region and the long, safe,
sandy beach at Fréjus-Plage is great for
youngsters. In 1913 the pioneer aviator,
Roland Garros, took off from here for his

epic eight-hour flight across the Mediterranean; Fréjus-Plage was the premier French naval airbase during World War I.

An ambitious marina development, Port-Fréjus, situated at the mouth of the River Argens was begun in 1989. When completed it will be able to accommodate 10 000 residents plus 700 boats and will undoubtedly further expand the activities of the town.

Fréjus marks the most westerly limit of the Esterel and the start of the **Massif des Maures**★★★ which reaches as far as Hyères. Though not as spectacular as the Esterel littoral, the coastline from Fréjus is relatively undeveloped and very pretty, with dozens of rocky inlets, secluded sandy bays and tiny hidden coves. Best of the public beaches is **La Nartelle** between **Les Issambres**★ and **Ste-Maxime**★★. Nicest of the towns is Ste-Maxime, facing St-Tropez across the bay. Popular as a bathing station at the end of the last century, it still has real character and a rather old-fashioned allure with a palm-fringed promenade, casino, a central sandy beach and an imposing new marina. Ten kilometres (6 miles) out of town on the D 25 to Le Muy, the **Musée du Phonographe et de la Musique Mécanique** (Phonographic Museum) contains a fascinating collection of over 300 mechanical music-makers dating from 1860.

**Port Grimaud**★ Do not be deterred by the mid-summer crowds and the fact that Port Grimaud attracts a million visitors a year; it is well worth a visit. A man-made, Provençal-style pleasure port, it was the first of many more recent marina projects all around the Mediterranean coast, and certainly the most

successful, having acquired a chic reputation and enthusiastic praise by the international boating community. Conceived as a reproduction fishing village based on the canals of Venice, the early buildings have

*The man-made pleasure port of Port Grimaud is popular among the boating fraternity.*

59

already taken on the patina of age and look remarkably authentic. The austere **church** in the main square features stained glass windows by Vasarely, and there are panoramic views of the port from the top of the bell tower. Now in its final construction stages, the complex consists of hotels, shops, restaurants and 2 500 waterside 'fishermen's cottages' and apartments with moorings for 700 boats.

**St-Tropez★★** For glamour and high style, the star of the Varois coastline is St-Tropez, the only really smart resort west of Cannes. First discovered by painter Paul Signac and writer friend Guy de Maupassant in 1892, when it

*An antique market in St-Tropez.*

*Brigitte Bardot starring in* And God Created Woman, *filmed in St-Tropez.*

was a fishing village unknown to tourists, St-Tropez quickly became popular with the French intellectual set. Used as the setting for the film *And God Created Woman*, St-Tropez's image and aura are late 20C, informal, trendy and – though the town is obviously cosmopolitan – basically very French indeed.

Although damaged by bombing in 1944, St-Tropez was faithfully reconstructed. Picturesque and pretty (there are few ugly or inappropriate additions), the town has a wonderfully authentic air. The pleasure **port★★** at **Quai Jean-Jaurès** lined with pretty painted red-tiled houses, busy bars and restaurants, and **Place des Lices**, with cafés, *pétanque* matches and a lively Provençal market on Tuesday and Saturday, are the focal points of activity in town. Behind the

*The painters of today continue a rich artistic tradition in St-Tropez.*

waterfront are the crowded shopping streets with some of the trendiest boutiques in France. Around the corner, the old quarter of La Ponche is quieter and a few fishing boats still bring in their early morning catch. The flamboyant 19C **Church**, crowned by an elegant wrought iron belltower, contains the bust of the town's patron saint. Above the old town a distinctive hexagonal mass of the **Citadel★** – home to preening peacocks – also houses a **Musée Naval** (Maritime Museum). But St-Tropez's real pride and glory is the **Musée de l'Annonciade★★** (Annonciade Museum), occupying a 16C chapel, where you can discover works representative of the major trends of the early 20C such as Pointillism with Signac (L'Orage), Fauvism (Matisse, Van Dongen, Friesz or Marquet), as well as Post Impressionists (Bonnard, Vallotton) and Expressionists (Chabaud or Rouault). Nearby, an amazing **Musée des**

**Papillons★** (Butterfly Museum) houses an astonishing collection of the son of the photographer J.-H. Lartigue.

Beach life is integral to the St-Tropez scene and the local **beaches★** are some of the loveliest on the Mediterranean. Closest to town are **Bouillabaisse** (a favourite with wind-surfers) and **Graniers**, but the in-crowd spurn these north-facing beaches on the Bay of St-Tropez in favour of the sublime stretch south of **Les Salins**. Legendary **Tahiti** and **Pampelonne** are where the 'beautiful people' go – perfect (paying) sandy beaches, backed by fields of vines.

The nearby hill-top villages on the St-Tropez peninsula are almost as fashionable as St-Tropez itself. **Gassin★**, with

*Shuttered windows and bougainvillaea in the charming village of Bormes-les-Mimosas, which is set on a hillside overlooking the sea.*

*The medieval village of Bormes-les-Mimosas.*

breathtaking **views★** over vineyards and pine woods to the sea on two sides, has been immaculately restored and has a choice of good restaurants, is popular for lunch or dinner out. Surrounded by vineyards, **Ramatuelle★** is a true Provençal village; not too over-preserved, it is well-known for its jazz festival in July. Only 5km (3 miles) from Tahiti and Pampelonne beaches, it makes a favoured alternative base.

## St-Tropez to Marseilles

The numerous resorts dotted along the coast westwards are, for the most part, post-war developments with good beaches but no special charm. **Le Lavandou★★**, the most important town on this stretch, is an old fishing village and one-time centre for cork production, now devoted to tourism. It has a busy port/marina and also offers more in the way of nightlife than neighbouring resorts. On the coast, the botanical domain of **Rayol★★**, with its exotic species of tropical trees, is definitely worth a visit. Just inland, the immaculately restored medieval village of **Bormes-les-Mimosas★**, occupying a splendid vantage point overlooking the bay, has quaint steep streets and panoramic coastal **views★**. Founded by pirates in 400 BC, the hill-top situation was also ideal for protection against pirate attacks in the 9C. Today Bormes is peaceful, perfumed and pretty – winner of the 'best floral village of France' award.

*Vineyards surround the town of Hyères.*

Because of its special micro-climate, mimosa has been intensively cultivated here since the 1920s and was added to the name in 1968. Port de Bormes is the marina serving the village with, on either side, two sandy public beaches: **Plage de la Favière** and **Plage de Cabasson**.

**Hyères★** The main road does not touch the coast around the Rade d'Hyères except at Port-de-Miramar which is an embarkation point for the offshore islands; Hyères is the only town of any size. Set in an agricultural area of vineyards and market gardens and now 5km (3 miles) inland due to silting up, it was once a thriving port. In 1254 St Louis stepped ashore here after one of his

*The Olbius-Riquier Gardens at Hyères.*

Crusades; the 13C church where he gave thanks for his safe return is on the main square, **Place de la République**. The new town of Hyères-les-Palmiers, developed in the 18C and 19C, was one of the oldest winter resorts on the Riviera, always a favourite with the French as well as the English. In the mid-1860s Hyères started specializing in the cultivation of palm trees and became the main producer in France. Palm trees line all the broad boulevards of Hyères, giving the town a markedly stately and exotic air. A wide variety of palms are still grown at the **Jardins Olbius-Riquier★** (Olbius-Riquier Gardens) – over 6ha (16 acres) of tropical and equatorial trees and plants.

The unprepossessing modern seaside town of Hyères-Plage and La Tour-Fondue on the **Giens Peninsula★★** south of Hyères are embarkation points for ferries (tourists are not allowed on the islands with their cars) to the lovely islands off Hyères. Ferries also leave from Le Lavandou, Cavalaire and Toulon.

**Iles d'Hyères★★★** (Hyères Islands) The archipelago off Hyères is one of the highlights of the western Riviera, especially for nature-lovers and walkers. Strung across the sea roughly parallel to the coast, they are also known as the golden islands on account of the metallic sheen on the glittering mica rock. Strategically placed, they have been coveted and fought over since time immemorial.

**Porquerolles★★★**, the most westerly and largest of the trio (7km long by 5km wide; 4 miles by 3 miles), belongs to the state and has been designated a conservation area to protect the eucalyptus and Umbrella Pine forests which, apart from some commercial vineyards, cover most of the island. Boats arrive at the harbour in the village of Porquerolles on the north coast which has a choice of hotels and restaurants, some of which are open all year. The island is traffic-free but there are bikes for hire and excellent **walks★★** on well-marked paths to the sandy beaches around the northern coast. The best is **Notre-Dame** – 3km (1.8 miles) away. Allow a couple of hours for the return cross-country trek to the lighthouse on the rugged south coast, from where there are panoramic **views★★** over the island. The gardens and glasshouses of the **Botanical Conservatory**, where research is carried out to ensure the survival of the island's flora, are open to the public. A small **museum** in Fort Sainte-Agathe documents the history of the islands.

*The main village on Port-Cros Island.*

Blanketed with dense vegetation, **Port-Cros**★★ is slightly smaller, wilder and almost mountainous with Mont Vinaigre the highest point at nearly 200m (656ft). Designated the National Park of Port-Cros, the island is a fully protected zone. Even bicycles are not allowed, there is no smoking outside the port area, flower-picking is strictly prohibited, and walkers must not stray off the official tracks. The conservation area extends out to sea, forming a rare nature reserve for land and marine life and migratory birds. Footpaths are clearly signposted from the landing stage at the village of Port-Cros – a botanical path follows the north coast to **La Palud Beach**★ and an **underwater path**★ is marked with buoys. The inland walk along the **Vallon de la Solitude**★ loops back via awesome cliffs on the southern shore and Route des Crêtes, with views out to sea. Alternatively, a leisurely

*The Mediterranean Sea with Port-Cros Island in the distance.*

10km (6 mile) march takes in Col de Port-Man and the east coast. For walkers wishing to stay over on Port-Cros, there is one fairly expensive hotel. Camping is absolutely forbidden.

The long twisting easterly island of **Levant** is partly occupied by a nudist village, Héliopolis, the rest being a military zone.

**Toulon★★ and Environs** A major port and home to the French fleet, Toulon was badly damaged during the last war and much of the city centre is functional but undeniably ugly, although some fine buildings have survived and there is a superb daily fish market. The city is unlikely to be a prime destination for most visitors but naval buffs should not miss the **Musée naval★** (Naval Museum) with its grand 17C entrance that was once the gateway to the city arsenal, and the **Musée du Vieux-Toulon** (Museum of Old Toulon) which highlights the life of Napoleon and his part in the defence of Toulon (1793).

Three main towns occupy the stretch towards Marseilles, each with its own particular personality. If you are looking for a coastal town that has retained some of its original identity and not been completely swallowed up by tourism, the cheerful fishing port of **Sanary-sur-Mer★** comes as an agreeable surprise. The colourful quayside – one of the prettiest on the Riviera – has as an unmistakable landmark, the slender 16C chapel of **Notre-Dame-de-Pitié** with direct access from the port. Picturesque pastel-tinted harbourside houses are flanked by stately palms, underneath which a lively fish and vegetable **market** takes place daily. In centuries past this was the foremost fishing port between Toulon and Marseilles. Diving

is popular and the small port of **Le Brusc** on the peninsula south of Sanary has become an international centre for this sport. For an interesting summer excursion, step on the ferry from Le Brusc for the 10-minute crossing to **Les Embiez★** – an island of diverse natural beauty belonging to the Paul-Ricard Foundation. Part of the foundation's marine research facility, the **Oceanographic Centre★**, is open to the public. The island also has a marina and produces its own wines.

Wine production is also an important activity around the port of **Bandol★★** 5km (3 miles) along the coast. Exceptionally sheltered and sunny, this is the major holiday resort between Toulon and Marseilles with three separate sandy **beaches** and a large yachting marina. Other attractions include a **casino**, tropical gardens and a **zoo**. For a fun day out, make a quick ferry trip to the

*Looking across Cassis and its coastline.*

privately owned offshore island of **Bendor**★ offering a fine beach, marina and a tasteful Provençal-style **tourist village** with craft shops and a cultural centre. Wine enthusiasts will want to browse around the unique **Exposition universelle des vins et spiritueux** (Universal Wine Exhibition) covering wine production in 45 countries.

Almost on the outskirts of Marseilles, the picturesque port of **Cassis**★ has long been a popular summer retreat. The bars that line the quayside are ideal for people- and boat-watching, especially **Bar de la Marine**. Something of an institution and favourite rendezvous for the locals and visitors from Marseilles, the 1930s décor has remained practically unchanged. No stop-over in Cassis would be complete without sampling

its famous **seafood**. With three good beaches, Cassis is a firm favourite and the port serves as the main departure point for boat trips around the spectacular *calanques*.

**Les Calanques★★** The coastline east of Marseilles is wild and semi-arid, typified by steep cliffs of startling pale limestone and narrow fjord-like inlets, known as *calanques*. Set within a classified and protected 5 000ha (12 355 acre) site, most of which is virtually inaccessible except on foot, the area remains remarkably preserved. Inevitably the sheer rock faces of the magnificent *calanque* cliffs are irresistible for keen climbers.

To admire the *calanques* in all their dramatic splendour, take the coastal road D 141 from La Ciotat (a pleasant seaside town, rather scarred by an enormous and very obvious offshore shipyard) to Cassis, via Cap Canaille, from where there are wonderful **views** westwards as far as Marseilles.

Few of the *calanques* can readily be reached by car but just west of Cassis, **Port-Miou** has vehicular access, as do Sormiou (where prehistoric **cave paintings** were discovered in an underwater cavern in 1991 – not open to the public) and **Morgiou**, near Marseilles. The parking is unguarded and notorious for theft, so be sure to leave no valuables in your car. Well-marked and scenic footpaths connect many of the *calanques* but the most popular way to view the coastline is from the sea. Boats leave the port at Cassis regularly throughout the day for trips lasting just under an hour.

**Marseilles★★★** The second largest city in France, Marseilles, with its exceptional **setting★★★**, is particularly stunning seen

*Les Calanques – a vertiginous marriage of white rock falling sharply to a sea constantly reflecting every shade of blue: nature as it was at the beginning of time!*

from the heights of **Notre-Dame-de-la-Garde**. The legendary **Vieux-Port★** (Old Port) and the picutresque **Quartier du Panier★** (Basket District) crowned by the **Vieille Charité Hospice★★**, which today houses museums, are pleasant areas to stroll around in... while waiting for your plane to leave!

## ON THE BEACH

With nearly 600km (373 miles) of coastline, a kind climate, virtually no tidal variation and a plethora of seaside scenes to choose from, the Riviera has something for everyone: super-sophistication, favourite family haunts, isolated inlets, bays of natural unspoilt beauty, watersport wonderlands and nudist hide-aways.

In general, coastal waters are remarkably pollution-free and a bacteria check is carried out every 15 days at certain control points. In addition, town councils of the main resorts are responsible for taking compulsory sea water analyses regularly. Results are displayed at the town hall (*mairie*). Public beaches are cleaned every morning and most have free shower facilities. Many provide a surveillance service and first-aid posts during the holiday season.

Public beaches are free but private beaches, run by professional concessionaires (*plagistes*), charge an entrance fee which is usually very reasonable, dependent on their official star rating of 1 to 4. The optional extras can, however, mount up: bar/restaurant service, cabins, sunbeds, parasols and so on, plus all the usual watersports. To make sea bathing as safe as possible, especially where there are also speed boat and water-skiing activities, buoys and flags clearly indicate swimming and non-swimming zones.

### Best Beaches

Even though the coastline from Cannes to
Menton – the original French Riviera –
includes some of the most fashionable and
select resorts, many beaches are composed
of pebbles and are not ideal for sunbathing
or swimming, although sand has been
imported on a few beaches. If you are
looking for glamour, and the chance of
some celebrity-spotting, try one of the
private beaches belonging to the luxury
hotels in **Cannes**, for example the Carlton,
Martinez or Majestic, all with imported sand.
Alternatively the public beach on the
Croisette is free but also sandy.

Most of **Monaco's** beaches have a sand

*Sunworshippers in
Nice. Beaches in
southern France are
clean with good
facilities.*

topping – Larvotto is the best public beach –
but for the ultimate in seaside
sophistication, buy daytime admission to the
ritzy Beach Plaza Hotel, at the eastern end of
Larvotto, complete with striped bathing
tents, giant-sized swimming pools, great
restaurants and every conceivable seasport.

For really chic sun-seeking, however,
**St-Tropez** is the place, though perhaps not
the townside north-facing beaches, such as
Graniers and Bouillabaisse. Trendy
sophisticates head south of Les Salines to
the 10km (6 miles) expanse of perfect sands,
set against a picturesque backdrop of
vineyards, that is the legendary beaches of
Tahiti and Pampelonne. The setting is
superb and facilities first-rate, including
plenty of smart bars and restaurants, but
prices are steep and nothing comes free
except the sunshine. For plenty of action
and nightlife, **Juan-les-Pins** is the place.

The best family beaches are around
**Hyères** where the slope is shallow and
therefore safe for young children. Popular
sandy beaches are found from Agay to
Fréjus-Plage, Cavalaire to Le Lavandou, and
the beaches around Port de Bormes. There's
plenty of space at Sanary and Bandol has a
choice of three beaches within walking
distance of the town.

If you want to get away from it all, head for
the coves between **St-Aygulf** and **Les
Issambres**, the *calanques* around **Cassis**, **Cap
Nègre** east of Le Lavandou or **Cap Sicié** west
of Toulon and the beaches of the Hyères
Islands, which are reached on foot! (*See* p.67)

The private beaches around the Baie des
Anges at **Nice** are the best for state-of-the-art
watersports, especially jet-skiing and
parasailing. Windsurfers congregate on

*L'Estagnol beach between Hyères and Le Lavandou. Some of the best family beaches are on this stretch of the coast.*

almost every beach and there are numerous accredited schools with qualified instructors. Favourite spots to catch the wind are Presqu'île de Giens and Ile de Porquerolles south of **Hyères**, Cap Sicié, Agay and Bouillabaisse beach at **St-Tropez**.

**Bendor Island** off Bandol is one of the largest scuba centres in Europe, and **La Busc**, south of Sanary, is also well known. Other sites rich in underwater life are the *calanques* around Cassis and the Hyères Islands. Specially equipped boats leave Cavalaire and Le Lavandou for deep-sea diving.

Although topless bathing is *de rigueur* in the South of France, totally nude bathing is forbidden on certain beaches but tolerated on others. The decision is entirely at the discretion of local councils so if in doubt ask at the nearest tourist office. Beaches where nude bathing is tolerated include: Le Layet east of Le Lavandou; Bonporteau on Pointe de la Nasque near Cavalaire; Blouch and Liberty at Ramatuelle; Capon at St-Tropez; La Pointe de l'Aiguille at Théoule sur-Mer; Salins beach at Hyères; and certain beaches on the west coast of Cap Ferrat.

## DAYS OUT IN THE COUNTRYSIDE

### The Nice Hinterland★★

Remote and massive, the mountainous hinterland behind Nice and Menton – the *arrière-pays* – is a world away from the clamour and congestion of the coast. Exploring this relatively unspoilt hinterland, where the panorama is breathtaking and life in isolated rural communities appears barely

*Houses in Sospel, showing the traditional trompe-l'œil murals.*

touched by the passage of time, is to discover another quite different, but no less beguiling, aspect of the Riviera.

## From Menton to the Col de Turini

Leave Menton by car or bus for a winding 15km (9 miles) journey to the interesting town of **Sospel★** straddling the banks of the River Bévéra, strategically placed at the junction of four mountain roads, on the ancient salt route and the major road from Nice to Turin. The town has a very Italian ambience and houses are brightly coloured with ornate façades. Look out particularly for the traditional *trompe-l'œil* **wall murals** – trick paintings realistically representing doors and windows that do not exist.

In the **medieval quarter**, approached by a wonderful 11C bridge, an arcaded central square is overlooked by the **church of St-Michel** with a 12C clock tower and altarpiece painted by François Bréa in 1530.

*A typical building in Sospel (above), and (below) the bridge that gives access to the medieval quarter.*

More recent are the beautifully preserved
authentic carriages with superb art-deco
interior from the luxurious Orient Express
train, which are on view at the railway station.
On a more sinister note, Sospel was directly
on the Maginot Line. Several forts surround
Sospel. St-Roch, built in 1934, is now a
**museum**. Fort du Barbonnet is also open for
guided visits in the summer.

To make a full day out, continue north on
the spectacular D 2566 for 15km (9 miles) to
Col de Turini at 1 607m (5 272ft). Half way
along, stop off at **Notre-Dame de-la-Menour**
– an isolated Romanesque church
approached by a formidable defensive wall
and an immense stone staircase. As a special
scenic 18km (11 miles) detour, take D 68

*Hill-top villages,
balconies over-
looking the sea
(here, Ste-Agnès),
where houses appear
to rise up out of the
rock...where time
seems to have
stopped, differing
changes in light
seemingly the only
witness to its
passing.*

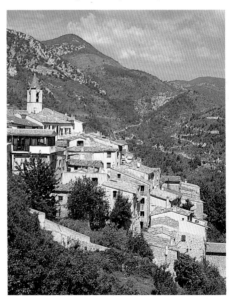

through the wonderful wooded scenery of the **Turini Forest**★★ to **L'Authion**★★ at 1 900m (6 234ft), where a War Memorial commemorates the site of bitter fighting in 1945. The road continues to climb to over 2 000m (6 562ft) with views to the Mercantour National Park to the north, before looping back to the Turini Pass.

Now head south to the winter ski resort of **Peïra-Cava**★ perched between two valleys: Bévéra and Vésubie. Just outside the village look out for a right turn to **La Pierre Plate**★★ with fantastic **views**★★, on a clear day, as far as the islands off the Cannes coast. Next come a string of typical mountain-top villages: the fortified medieval village of **Lucéram**★; **L'Escarène** with the 15C church of Ste-Marguerite containing many important paintings and art treasures; **Peillon**★★ with impressive frescoes in the chapel of the Pénitents Blancs; **Peille**★ with views over the Baie des Anges; and **Ste-Agnès**★, pretty but rather touristic and the highest of the villages in this corner. **Gorbio**★, set amongst olive groves, is well known for the Fête des Limaces in early June when, as evening falls, the village is decorated by the light of thousands of oil-filled snail shells. From Gorbio, it is no more than a few minutes' drive back to the coast at either Menton or Monaco.

## From Nice to the Vésubie, Tinée and Var Valleys

Head out of Nice on RN 202 – the highway that leads directly north beside the River Var – for 30km (19 miles) to Plan-du-Var. To explore the Vésubie Valley, turn right on D 2562 through a steep-sided gorge to St-Jean-la-Rivière and left on D 32 to **Utelle**★; as the road climbs there are wonderful **views**

*An ornate wooden carving on the door of the church in Utelle.*

*The isolated town of Utelle.*

over dense pine forests back down the gorge. Perched on a mountainside at 800m (2 625ft), Utelle is an isolated and ancient town that has lost none of its unique character. See the lovely square with its tinkling fountain and the splendid **church of St-Véran**.

Continue climbing for 6km (3½ miles) to **La Madone d'Utelle** at nearly 1 200m (3 937ft). This simple chapel, built in 850 as a sanctuary and place of pilgrimage, and restored in the 19C, is often shrouded in cloud, but the **panoramic vistas★★★** on a clear day are remarkable.

The options now, both equally scenic, are to continue on D 32 and across the Tinée Valley or to return to St-Jean and follow the Vésubie River north through Lantosque and Roquebillière, up onto the high Alpine pastures and the medieval town of **St-Martin-**

*The fortified walls of Entrevaux.*

**Vésubie★**, now a popular mountain resort offering excellent walking and climbing. You could then make an 8km (5 mile) detour up to the resort of **Le Boréon★★** with its spectacular waterfall where the river plunges 40m (131ft) into a narrow gorge, and then drive back over Col St-Martin to the Tinée Valley and D 2205 to Nice.

Alternatively, from Plan-du-Var continue on RN 202, following the River Var for 40km (25 miles), passing through the pleasant market town of **Puget-Théniers★** to the historic city of **Entrevaux★**, a perfectly preserved and atmospheric **medieval town★** with original ramparts, three drawbridges and a hill-top citadel approached by a series of fortified gates. Surrounded by olive groves reputed to be centuries old and strategically placed on the border between Provence and

*Detail of one of the restored town gates of Entrevaux.*

the county of Nice, Entrevaux was an important frontier post and always part of France, whilst neighbouring Puget-Thèniers, just 7km (4 miles) away, belonged to the Dukes of Savoy. The **views★** from the citadel are well worth the walk to the top, which starts at the automatic entrance gate – you will need a 10F piece – behind the Town Hall (*mairie*).

Stop in Entrevaux, have lunch, browse around the narrow maze of streets and visit the Flamboyant **cathedral** then carry on on RN 202 for 4km (2½ miles) and turn right through the spectacular red-rock **Daluis Gorges★★** to the little mountain town of Guillaumes and on to the year-round resort of Valberg at 1 700m (5 578ft). At Beuil, turn south through the awesome **Cians Gorges★★★** where the river drops 1 600m (5 250ft) in 25km (15½ miles), and back onto RN 202

and the road to Nice. If time allows, call in at
**Touët-sur-Var★** and walk up to the rather
forbidding old village, seat of the brutal and
unruly Lords of Beuil. Look in at the unusual
church, built over a stream that rushes
beneath grilling that runs down the centre
aisle. The round trip will take a full day but
for a visit to Entrevaux only, allow just over
one hour each way. Alternatively, take the
narrow gauge railway to Entrevaux from
Gare du Sud (a 15-20-minute walk from the
mainline station in Nice).

## From Cannes to the Verdon Gorges
Unquestionably one of the greatest
natural phenomena in Europe, the **Verdon
Gorges★★★** are exceptional and definitely a
spectacle not to be missed, even though at

*The stunning red-rock Gorges de Daluis.*

260km (162 miles) for the round trip it is a long day out from Cannes. Carved out of limestone rock by the Verdon River and its tributaries, the gigantic chasm is 21km (13 miles) long and in parts reaches 700m (2 297ft) in depth. Remote and wild, the length of the gorge was only properly explored in 1905. Running from east to west with roads on the north and south sides, a complete round tour is possible in a full day out. However, allow sufficient time as these are not roads that can be rushed. Likewise it is unwise to contemplate the trip in mid-winter.

Leave Cannes on the old **Route Napoléon★★** that passes through Grasse and then to **Castellane★** – a busy market town and popular tourist centre as 'gateway' to the Verdon Grand Canyon. Call in at the Tourist Office to pick up further information. Take D 952 beside the River Verdon to the road junction at Pont-de-Soleils and continue on D 952 which follows the northern edge of the gorge. Stop off at **Point Sublime★★★** offering stupendous views and head for La Palud-sur-Verdon. Just before reaching the village, there is a choice between a worthwhile 23km (14 mile) detour **Route des Crêtes★★★** (D 23), built in 1973 to allow vehicles to follow the contours of the canyon, or cutting across country directly to the attractive tourist town at the head of the gorge, **Moustiers-Ste-Marie★★**. Strikingly situated beneath a craggy ravine over which a five-pointed golden star has been dramatically strung since the 13C, Moustiers is a traditional pottery town famed for its delicate highly glazed 18C-style faïence which is on sale in many specialist shops. Original examples of the work are displayed in the Pottery Museum.

*The Verdon Gorges – amid the silence of a wild and awe-inspiring country-side, cut into by waters of a supernatural green, a return to essentials, far from the hubbub of today's world.*

*The untouched beauty of the Massif des Maures.*

On the return leg, the D 957 skirts **Ste-Croix Lake★★**, a vast man-made lake into which the Verdon River now flows, before joining the **Corniche Sublime★★★** D 71, the southern route that was constructed in 1947 to allow the gorge to be opened up to visitors. From here D 71 strikes out across country via **Comps-sur-Artuby** to rejoin Route Napoléon 20km (12 miles) south of Castellane.

### From St-Tropez around the Massif des Maures

The **Maures Mountains★★★**, nearly 60km (37 miles) long and 40km (25 miles) wide, are clad in cork oaks, sweet chestnuts, umbrella and Aleppo pines. To discover their dramatic unspoilt beauty, head for **Grimaud★** – a delightful chateau-capped hill-top village with glorious views from **Place**

*La Croix des Maures above La Garde-Freinet.*

**du Château**. (A little tourist-tram train operates from here to and from Port Grimaud on the coast.) During the 11C the village was a base of the Knights Templar but the well-preserved house on Rue des Templiers sadly is not open to the public. See instead the **arcaded houses** designed to be closed up at times of attack and the 11C **Church of St-Michel**. Then follow the scenic twisting road through woods of cork oaks, recognizable by their bark-stripped trunks, up to **La Garde-Freinet** – ancient stronghold of the Saracens during the 9C and 10C. (The ruined Saracen castle is half an hour's walk from the village.) For a short tour, take the road east over Col de Vignon with tantalizing glimpses of the distant sea, to the wine town of Plan-de-la-Tour and down to Ste-Maxime.

For a full day out, take the route west to Col des Fourches with an optional well-marked detour to the highest point of the Massif des Maures at 780m (2 559ft), and **Notre-Dame-des-Anges★** – an isolated 19C chapel full of votive offerings. This spot, with its unrivalled views in all directions, has been a place of worship since the 6C when the son of Clovis built the first church as thanks for victory over the Visigoths. Now head south to **Collobrières**, main centre of the Massif des Maures, surrounded by forests of sweet chestnuts and famed for its crystallized chestnuts, (*marrons glacés*). Chestnut products are on sale in shops and stalls but actually to see the manufacturing processes you will have to come during the Chestnut Festival in mid-October. Collobrières is also the centre of the local wine production and offers free wine-tastings during the country market held on the second Sunday in December.

From Collobrières either continue south to Le Lavandou; cut across country on D 14 via Col de Taillade back to Grimaud; or, if you have had your fill of spectacular mountain roads, opt for RN 98 via La Mole to **Cogolin**, a

*A pipe shop display in Cogolin which specializes in making briar pipes (below left).*

*Sweet chestnuts in the Massif des Maures (below).*

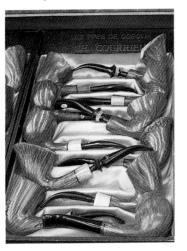

craft town and centre for traditional briar pipe-making, the construction of reeds for woodwind instruments and for top-quality hand-made carpets. Many **workshops** can be visited: ask for details at the tourist office.

## The Wine Route from Cassis and Bandol

Although most areas in the South of France are knee-deep in vines, the wines produced around Cassis and Bandol are amongst the most sought after, and many of the vineyards themselves are located in remarkable coastal scenery. The following circuit takes about half a day, or longer if you stop off for lunch and perhaps a few tastings (*dégustations*) and/or purchases along the way.

Because of the geographical position of Cassis in a bowl facing the sea, the steeply terraced vineyards start at the outskirts of the town. Take the road to Marseilles and turn right almost immediately on D 1 to La Bédoule. You will pass various viticultural *domaines* and have memorable views over vineyards towards the sea and Cap Canaille. Continue on D 1, passing under the autoroute, and before reaching the pass at Col de l'Ange, turn right on D 3 to La Bégude and Le Camp du Castellet, where you should turn right to **Le Castellet★**. This is an interesting medieval wine village with more fine views over vineyards and the sea. It was here in the *Tante Marie* bar that the internationally acclaimed popular French novelist/director Marcel Pagnol filmed *La Femme du Boulanger* in 1938. Carry on south for 3km (2 miles) to the wine town of **Le Beausset**, taking time to look at the Romanesque **Chapel N.-D.-du-Beausset-Vieux** and the interior of the much newer

**church** which contains fine paintings by the Marseilles painter Michel Serre (1658-1733). Continue south on N 8 through vineyard country to the wine towns of Ste-Anne-d'Evanos and Ollioules, where you turn off onto D 220 along the spectacular Massif du Gros-Cerveau, and into **Bandol★★**. This busy seaside resort with an animated marina is the centre of the local wine industry so be sure to call in at the Maison des Vins, on the waterfront next to the Tourist Office, where a selection of local producers' wines are on sale. The streets behind the port are packed with restaurants so this would be a good place to lunch. Alternatively, head into the hills to **La Cadière-d'Azur**, another historic hill-top wine village, with a reputation for good food as well as fine wines.

Depending on time and inclination, you could either return to Cassis via the autoroute – there is an exit just outside La Cadière-d'Azur – or meander round the coast via Les Lecques.

*A trellissed grapevine (above left).*

*An example of local craft produce (above right).*

## FAMILY OUTINGS

If you need a break from the beach, head inland to the mountains behind Nice where the ski resorts of **Auron★**, **Isola 2000★★** and **Valberg★** offer year-round facilities: cross-country and Alpine skiing in winter; mountain biking, pony trekking and rambling on the *pistes* and hillsides during summer. Or go inland from Cannes along Route Napoléon to **Lake Ste-Croix★★**, a vast man-made lake offering every kind of watersport, situated at the head of the spectacular Verdon Gorges.

### Aquatic Attractions

**Marineland★** at Antibes is full of interest. A superb complex of water-orientated attractions, it features a marine zoo with penguins, seal and performing dolphins and orca (killer) whales, plus **Aquasplash** – a water playground with giant toboggans and wave machines. Other water game parks are **Aquatica** at Fréjus, **Niagara** at La Mole near Cavalaire and **Aqualand** at St-Cyr-sur-Mer near Toulon.

Still on a watery theme, there is a much-acclaimed **Oceanographic Museum★★★** at Monaco (*see* p.35), consisting of 90 enormous aquaria featuring every aspect of underwater flora and fauna. **Foundation Ricard★** on the island of Les Embiez near Toulon (reached by ferry from La Brusc) is concerned with marine research and aquaculture. Yet another way to discover the marine underworld is to board the observation submarines (with a transparent hull) that explore the coastal waters.

### Boat Trips

For more conventional sea trips, boats leave

the marine station (*gare maritime*) beside the Croisette at Cannes for visits to the unspoilt islands of **Ste-Marguerite**★★ (15 minutes), and **St-Honorat**★★ (30 minutes).

*There is always plenty for children to do, such as these pony rides in Jardins Olbius-Riquier, Hyères.*

The finest views of the lovely coastline around Toulon are best seen from the cruisers that leave from quay Cronstadt. The most spectacular of the many trips from the Old Port at St-Raphaël is the one by catamaran around the **Esterel coast**★★★.

Boats leave the port at Cassis to tour the unique **calanques**★★, the rocky inlets east of Marseilles (*see* p.73). From Presqu'île de Giens near Hyères boats go to the offshore islands of **Ile de Port-Cros**★★, which is a protected national park (*see* p.69); and to **Ile de Porquerolles**★★★ with pretty coves and small beaches (*see* p.67).

## Other Treats

Animal parks make a great day out for the entire family. Choose from **zoos** at Cap Ferrat, Sanary-sur-Mer and Toulon, where the zoo is on Mont Faron and can be reached by cable car; a **safari park**★ at Fréjus; a **tropical bird reserve** (Jardin d'Oiseaux tropicaux) at La Londe near Hyères; and a **Tortoise Village** (Villages des Tortues) at Gonfaron, inland from St-Tropez. Tiny tots will love **La Petite Ferme** at Antibes, a mini-farm with lots of baby animals to bottle-feed, pony rides, a mouse village and the chance to see chicks hatching.

## LIVING THE CÔTE D'AZUR LIFE

In order to appreciate the Côte d'Azur, and Provence in general, forget for once the hectic rhythm of city life and follow the example of the locals. Throughout its villages you will come across the young and the old sitting at pavement cafés, making sure they're well out of the sun. They have no doubt ordered the inevitable *pastis* and, while picking at a few black olives, are in deep discussion about the truly important things in this, their world: the morning's fishing catch, or maybe the latest performance of the local football team. Further away on a shady avenue, a small crowd is watching a game of *pétanque* with an expert eye, a pretext for endless discussion: the position of the balls is measured, contested, measured again until, following a perfect *carreau*, a virtuoso player ends up turning the tables.

You will want to take time to wander through the colourful markets which take over towns and villages for a morning or a day: fruits and vegetables, aromatic herbs, marinated olives, spices, honey and local specialities, cut flowers, handicrafts, printed fabrics – as much a pleasure for the ear as the eye. The bustle and noise creates a picturesque *bon enfant* atmosphere, to which the singsong accent and a smattering of Provençal words – which never fail to be appreciated by those who understand French, even if there's nothing conventional about the French spoken here – merely contribute.

Lightly tanned by the sun's rays, warm even in the midst of winter, dazzled by this light which so attracts and inspires artists, by this often exhuberant vegetation where Mimosa, Cyprus, Eucalyptus, Olive, Almond and Pine trees mingle with even more exotic species, mouth-watering from the aromas of this local cooking which, seeming to fear blandness more than anything else, passionately introduces mixtures of the hottest of spices, under the spell of this sea which, passing from deep blue to indigo to emerald green, temptingly calls out to the passer-by, you will no doubt understand how the Côte d'Azur has managed to capture and retain the attention of so many artists, wealthy travellers of by-gone years. English lords, grand Russian princes or American millionaires.

Why not follow in the footsteps of Lord Brougham, the English 'inventor' of Cannes, of Somerset Maugham, of D. H. Lawrence, of F. J. Gould or of the Czarina Alexandra Fedorovna? Do you perhaps regret that the Côte d'Azur may have fallen victim to its success: real-estate projects disfiguring the picturesque former fishing ports, the coasline from Cannes to Menton seemingly to have become one continuous town...If so, then all that's needed is to go off in search of authenticity – to the hill-top villages of the surrounding *niçois* hinterland or to the Esterel mountains, to the fabulous unspoilt Îles d'Or (Golden Islands) or the exquisite *Calanques*, or colourful fishing boats dancing on the transparent waters.

It's then, in front of a serving of gurnard (*rouget de roche*), of grilled bas (*loup grillé*), an *aïoli* or perhaps a copious *bouillabaisse*, whilst savouring a white Cassis wine or a Bandol rosé, touched by the peacefulness of the moment and the pleasure of the *farniente*, such is the real Provençal in its *cabanon*, that you will be surprised to find yourself replying to whoever suggests an afternoon activity 'aujourd'hui peut-être...'

## WEATHER

The seductive Mediterranean climate has always been a major factor in the year-round appeal of the South of France. The region can count on up to 2 900 hours of sunshine per year – the highest number in France – peaking in July with around ten hours daily. The typical seasonal pattern is long, hot, dry summers and short, mild winters. Most of the rain – on average no more than 900mm (35in) per year – falls during spring and autumn.

Especially windy weather is not characteristic, with the exception of pleasant easterly sea breezes that temper the coastline heat in summer, and the infamous Mistral which periodically blows down the Rhône Valley and across Provence. The effects of the Mistral are most pronounced in the west and it is particularly active in early spring when wind speeds of over 140kph (85mph) are not unusual. Vicious it may be while it lasts, but invariably radiant sunshine and brilliant blue skies follow, combined with a remarkable clarity and luminosity.

High season is July and August when the weather is at its most intense. Mid-day land temperatures soar to the mid-30s°C, with sea temperatures around 26°C. Humidity levels can be equally high and it is not until nine or ten o'clock at night that the air begins to feel noticeably cooler.

By contrast the weather during the months either side – May/June and September/October – may be less predictable but are also more comfortable for many tastes. Although daytime temperatures are usually still very warm, in the mid-20s°C, showers are more prevalent and storms are possible, especially in late summer. Evenings tend to be much cooler and outside dining may not be possible in May and October.

Winters are usually sunny and relatively mild, although a little snow is possible in particularly hard years. Temperatures can fall to around freezing at night but ice and frost are only common inland. Excellent skiing is available from

December to March in the mountain resorts about two hours' drive from Nice.

## CALENDAR OF EVENTS

In addition to the events listed below, every town and village celebrates its particular patron saint's day with processions, *boules* competitions, children's games and dances.

### January

**Mid-month** *Monte-Carlo Rally* – one of the most important motor rallies, attracting top drivers; day and night tests on roads in the mountains behind Monaco.
**Late January or early February** *Monaco Circus Festival* – featuring major international performers.

### February

**February and early March** *Carnaval de Nice* – with processions, floats, battles of flowers and firework displays.
**Last two weeks** *Lemon Festival* in Menton – colourful displays decorated with oranges and lemons, floats and firework displays.
**3rd Sunday** *Mimosa Festival* in Bormes-les-Mimosas.

### March

**Early March** *Violet Festival* in Tourettes-sur-Loup, near Vence.

### April

**1st two weeks** *International Flower Festival*, Cagnes-sur-Mer.

**Easter** *Procession du Christ Mort* in Roquebrune-Cap-Martin.
**Easter Sunday and Monday** *Carnival and Battle of Flowers* in Vence.
**Easter Monday** *Pilgrimage* to the isolated Chapel of La Madonne in Utelle, north of Nice.

### May

**Mid-month** *Grasse Rose Festival.*
**16-19 May** *St-Tropez Bravades* – rumbustious and colourful costumed processions dating from the 12C.
**Two weeks mid-month** *Cannes: International Film Festival.*
**Sunday after Ascension** *Monaco Grand Prix* – Formula One race around the streets of Monaco.

### June

**15 June** *St-Tropez 2nd Bravade* Fête des Espagnols – celebrating naval victories over the Spanish in 1637.
**Mid-month** *Bormes-les-Mimosas Flower Festival.*
**Throughout the month** *Le Lavandou Craft Festival.*

### July

**14 July** – festivities and fireworks celebrating *National Day* (Bastille Day) in all towns and villages.
*Bullfight* (*corrida*) in the Roman arena of Fréjus.
*Nice Jazz Festival* – in the gardens of the Roman arena at Cimiez (☎ 04 93 87 16 28).
**Mid-month World Jazz Festival**, Juan-les-Pins (☎ 04 92 90 53 00).

### August

**5 August** *Passion Procession* in Roquebrune-Cap-Martin.

**1st weekend** *Grasse Jasmine Festival*; *Vallauris: Pottery Fair*.
**1st two weeks** *Festival Lyrique* at Thoronet Abbey.
**15 August** *Bullfight* in Fréjus.
**Throughout the month** *Jazz Festival* in Ramatuelle, and *Chamber Music Festival* in Menton.

## September
**First weekend** *Festin des baguettes* in Peille.
*Régates Royales* in Cannes.

## October
**First weekend** *Olive Tree Festival* in Ollioules.
**23 October** *Chestnut Festival* in La Garde-Freinet.

**Last two weeks** *Chestnut Festival* in Collobrières.

## November
**Throughout month** *Chestnut Festival* in Gonfaron.
**19 November** *Monaco National Day* – celebrated with an impressive firework display.
**Last week** *Cannes International Dance Festival* – featuring contemporary dance and ballet.

## December
**1st two weeks** *Santon Fair* in Marseilles (*La Canebière*); also at Toulon, Fréjus, La Garde-Freinet, Bormes-les-Mimosas...
**1st week** *Bandol Wine Festival*.

*Ceramics from Vallauris on traditional Provençal fabric.*

## ACCOMMODATION

The French Riviera can be very expensive if you choose the smarter coastal resorts as your base – but away from the coast, prices are much more modest.

Hotels are graded by the French tourist ministry from one to four stars, with an average comfortable two-star hotel costing from 260-380F for a room for two; breakfast is usually extra at about 25-50F per person. Some hotels levy a daily tax of 3-6F.

### Recommendations

The *Michelin Red Guide France* lists a selection of hotels. Here are just a few recommendations:

**Bandol**
*Hôtel la Ker-Mocotte* 193 Rue Raimu. Small hotel opposite the casino. Formerly the villa belonging to the actor Raimu, decorated with old film posters. Direct access to the beach. Fairly expensive.

**Beaulieu-sur-Mer**
*Réserve de Beaulieu* Bd du Maréchal Leclerc ☎ **04 93 01 00 01**, Fax 04 93 01 28 99.
A Florentine palace by the sea. Lucurious, with good food. Very expensive, naturally!

**Cannes**
*Hôtel Albert 1er* 68 Av de Grasse ☎ **04 93 39 24 04**, Fax 04 93 38 83 75. Very old house in a quiet area.
*Hôtel Florian* 8 Rue du Cdt André ☎ **04 93 39 24 82**,Fax 04 93 99 18 30. Near la Croisette. Family hotel with every comfort.
*Hôtel Lutetia* 6 Rue Michel-Ange

☎ **04 93 39 35 74**. An unpretentious hotel with a welcoming atmosphere in a quiet side-street.
**Èze**
*Auberge des Deux Corniches* Rte du Col d'Èze ☎ **04 93 41 19 54**. A simple country inn with shady terrace and pretty view of the sea.
**Gourdon**
*Auberge de Courmes* 3 Rue des Platanes à Courmes ☎ **04 93 77 64 70**. A charming village across the way from the Loup Gorges: such is the setting for this country inn, very simple and quiet.
**Mougins**
*Manoir de l'Étang* Route d'Antibes ☎ **04 93 90 01 07**, Fax 04 92 92 20 70. Very quiet, isolated, in parkland.

*Market stalls provide delicious fruit.*

**Nice**

*Hôtel Durante* 16 Av Durante
☎ 04 93 88 84 40, Fax 04 93 87 77 76. Near the town centre, quiet hotel with its own garden.

*Hôtel la Pérouse* 11 Quai Rauba-Capèu ☎ 04 93 62 34 16. At the foot of a château, with a clear view of the Bay of Angels.

**Peillon**

*Auberge de la Madone* ☎ 04 93 79 91 17. An inn for those who like to take the time to live... Superb views. Rooms from 550F.

**Port-Cros**

*Hôtel Manoir* ☎ 04 94 05 90 52. An address full of charm: a 1930s villa in extensive grounds, a world away from the mainland and the bustle of daily life.

**Ramatuelle**

*Chez Camille* ☎ 04 94 79 80 38. Family-run hotel since 1912. Opposite the sea – seafood a speciality.

**St-Jean-Cap-Ferrat**

*Hôtel Frégate* ☎ 04 93 76 04 51. A simple hotel a stone's throw from the public beach.

**St-Martin-Vésubie**

*Châtaigneraie* ☎ 04 93 03 21 22. A house within a park, an ideal opportunity to discover the Mercantor Park, or to simply relax in the country.

**St-Paul-de-Vence**

*La Colombe d'Or* ☎ 04 93 32 80 02, Fax 04 93 32 77 78. Provençal style. Famous for its modern paintings and sculptures. Expensive.

*A market vendor selling local grapes.*

*Le Hameau* 1km along the Colle-sur-Loup road ☎ **04 93 32 80 24**. A former farm transformed into a hotel.

**St-Tropez**

*Hôtel Lou Cagnard* Av P. Roussel ☎ **04 94 97 04 24**, Fax 04 94 97 09 44. Small hotel, no restaurant, in the centre of town. Reasonably priced.

**Tourrettes-sur-Loup**

*Résidence des Chevaliers* Rue Caire ☎ **04 93 59 31 97**. Set on the side of a mountain, experience the superb view from Antibes to Monaco. The view alone justifies the price of rooms (550F).

*For other types of accommodation, see the Accommodation section on p. 112.*

## FOOD AND DRINK

The food of southern France is essentially sunshine food, a healthy Mediterranean diet based on olive oil with plenty of assorted **fish**, such as various types of sea bream and mullet, and hog-fish (*rascasse*), an essential ingredient in the preparation of the famous bouillabaisse. You should also take advantage of your stay by enjoying an *aïoli*, originally a local variation of mayonnaise heavily perfumed with garlic. Served as an accompaniment with boiled cod (*morue bouillie*) and vegetables, it has given its name to this dish which is never more apreciated than when shared between a group of friends in the summer. You can try it in August at Entecasteaux (9th), Collobrières (12th-16th) or at Fayence (26th-28th) by making a reservation through the Tourist Office – a convivial atmosphere for a meal that will remain, without a shadow of doubt, one of the lasting souvenirs of your stay!

There are also delicious roast or braised **meats**, with lamb being the most popular, the best reputed to

*Take your time eating and drinking in southern France. The ambiance lends itself to leisurely snacks and meal-times. This is Rue Masséna in Nice.*

come from Sisteron in Haute Provence or the salt marshes of Camargue. Taste it at its succulent best as *gigot d'agneau* – leg of lamb roast with garlic and herbs.

**Vegetables** are one of the glories of southern French cooking. The world renowned vegetable dish *ratatouille* – a *ragout* of vegetables – will taste even finer made on its native soil. Peppers are also wonderful when oven-roasted, skinned and then left to cool in olive oil (*poivrons au four*).

There are many **pasta** restaurants in southern France, especially around Nice. Ravioli and cannelloni are the favourites, invariably served with a tomato sauce and sprinkled with grated cheese. Pizzas are sold everywhere,

but in the Nice area watch out for the chili peppered pizza oil.

With so much luscious **fruit** available, it is hardly surprising that rich creamy desserts have never played a major role in local cuisine. *Tarte au citron* – a tangy lemon pie – is a great favourite and because of the climate and the Italian connection ices and sorbets are much in demand.

In past decades, the **wines** of southern France were often scorned, but this is not the case any more. The real speciality of the region is its pale pink *rosé*. Light, dry and very easy to drink, *rosé* is perfect as an aperitif, or to accompany a light lunch or meal of pasta. Even those who would not dream of drinking *rosé* back home, will find that they completely suit the ambience, climate and food on site. Some of the very best *rosés* come from the vineyards around St-Tropez.

In wine-growing areas, the local wines are often sold inexpensively in a *carafe* or *pichet*, rather than a bottle, and are usually excellent. If you also want water to accompany your meal, ask for a *carafe d'eau*, which will be a jug of tap water which is free. You will have to pay for bottled water – *eau minérale*.

Wining and dining is one of the great pleasures of southern France. Prices can be very reasonable and during the summer months lunches are served in the sunshine under large parasols. Romantic candle-lit dinners are taken under the stars.

A meal is expected to include at least three courses and all restaurants offer a choice of *table d'hôte* menus with a starter, main course and cheese and/or dessert (dessert is always served after the cheese). These set menus generally represent better value than dishes from the *à la carte* selection, especially at lunchtime when prices are often reduced.

Except in the very up-market and expensive restaurants, dress is casual but should be reasonably smart. Well-behaved children are always welcome and some restaurants offer an inexpensive *menu d'enfant*.

The *Michelin Red Guide France* lists a selection of restaurants. Here are just a few recommendations. The prices indicated correspond to the price of menus per person.

*Window shopping in Nice, at Galeries Lafayette.*

## Antibes

*L'Oursin* 16 Rue République
☎ 04 93 34 13 46. Fish from the
day's catch, in the heart of town.
A restaurant much appreciated by
local residents (99F).

*Chez les Poissonniers* 16 Cours
Masséna ☎ 04 93 34 23 10.
A fish shop? You could be forgiven
for thinking so on discovering this
stall opposite the market! In fact,
it's a restaurant – and a popular
one too (136/164F).

## Bandol

*Réserve* ☎ 04 94 29 30 13.
Just out of town, on the coast
(135/390F).

## Biot

*Les Terraillers* 11 Rte Chemin-Neuf
☎ 04 93 65 01 50. In a 16C
potter's workshop, a cuisine with
southern accents (250/360F).

## Bormes-les-Mimosas

*Lou Portaou* Rue Cubert des Poètes
☎ 04 94 64 86 37. Set in an
ancient tower (178F).

## Cannes

*Brun* 2 Rue Louis Blanc ☎ 04 93
39 98 94. Facing the port, a
favourite of fish and seafood
enthusiasts (170/230F).

*Belle Otéro* 58 Bd de la Croisette, on
the 7th floor of the Carlton
☎ 04 93 99 51 10. Want to splash
out one evening? A *grande table*
where you'll feel like a star...for the
duration of a dinner (410/620F).

## Menton

*Oh! Matelot!* Pl Loredan-Larchey
☎ 04 93 28 45 40. A dream for
children, who love the boat decor
and board games. Buffet formula.
*A Braijade Méridiounale* 66 Rue

Hand-made wicker baskets for sale.

Longue ☎ 04 93 35 65 65. Local
cuisine and grills in the side-streets
of Old Menton (125/285F).

## Monaco

*Café de Paris* Place du Casino
☎ (00-377) 92 16 20 20. A 1930s
style café – ideal before trying your
luck at the casino across the
way...or celebrating your new-
found fortune (200/450F)!

## Nice

*La Tapenade* 6 Rue Ste-Réparate
☎ 04 93 80 65 63. In the heart of
Old Nice, a cosy decor for tasing
local specialities, simply prepared
(89/130F).

*L'Escalinada* 22 Rue Pairolières
☎ 04 93 62 11 71. One of Old
Nice's traditional addresses
(110/125F).

*Bocaccio* 7 Rue Masséna ☎ 04 93
87 71 76. On a pedestrian walkway,
decorated in Mediterranean
nautical style (140/200F).

*Coco Beach* 2 Av Jean-Lorrain

*The unique tropézienne sandals.*

☎ **04 93 89 39 26**. A former fishing cabin with a clear view of the port, serving seafood (260/380F).

**Ramatuelle**
*Leï Salins* Plage des Salins
☎ **04 94 97 04 40**. Facing the sea, fresh fish of the day grilled in front of you (135/260F).

**St-Tropez**
*La Table du Marché* 38 Rue Georges Clémenceau ☎ **04 94 97 85 20**. A 'delicatessen-bistro' two steps away from the Place des Lices (149/320F).
*Leï Mouscardins* On the port (Tour du Portalet). Southern flavours and sea views. Connoisseurs, take note (335F)!

**Villefranche-sur-Mer**
*Mère Germaine* Quai Courbet
☎ **04 93 01 71 39**. Near the harbour, in local style (210/280F).

## SHOPPING

In the South of France, a lunch break of two, three or even four hours from noon is usual, especially during summer. In the main cities and large towns, a few department stores and most shopping malls remain open throughout the day; out-of-town hypermarkets also open from 9-10am to 8-9pm (later in summer), Monday to Saturday. Otherwise, the midday siesta is sacrosanct! Town centre shops open from 9am to noon and 2-4pm till 7-8pm Monday to Saturday. Food shops open an hour or two earlier and also open Sunday morning; but often close on Monday. Shops in rural areas open Sunday morning too and take a day off during the week.

Once opening hours are sorted

out, the choice of both venue and goods available is enormous. For general requirements, head for the vast out-of-town **hypermarkets** (*hypermarchés*) with a truly amazing range of foodstuffs, clothes and household items at down-to-earth prices. Such complexes often also house up to a couple of hundred supplementary shops and restaurants all under one roof and have extensive free parking.

## Luxury Goods

For every conceivable kind of luxury goods and international designer brand names, the smart boutiques on Rue de France in Nice, Rue d'Antibes in Cannes, and central Monte-Carlo around the Casino are the places to go; but the trendiest designer clothes are found in the ultra-chic boutiques of St-Tropez. Up-market department stores such as Galeries Lafayette, situated on the main streets of Nice, Toulon and Marseilles, are another happy hunting ground. They stock many designer labels and have excellent perfumery and cosmetic counters.

## Arts and Crafts

Artists and craftsmen have long been attracted to the delights of living and working in the South of France, but lately there has been renewed interest in traditional Provençal crafts. **Craft fairs** (*foires artisanales*) are regular events in many towns; and in most coastal resorts, artists set up pavement stalls on warm summer evenings.

Certain towns and villages have acquired a reputation as art and craft centres. The hilltop village of **St-Paul-de-Vence**, for example, has lured painters since the last century. Nearby **Tourettes-sur-Loup** has potters, weavers, silk-painters, jewellers and wood-carvers. Vence and Mougins, where Picasso spent the last years of his life, are acclaimed for their studios and galleries.

**Vallauris**, inland from Antibes, has been a **pottery** town since Roman times and today over 100 pottery workshops offer a complete range of ceramic ware, from cheap and cheerful to sophisticated and pricey. Next door, **Biot** has a tradition of **glass-making**, and blowers continue to produce distinctive bubble-effect handmade glassware.

**Cogolin** is well-known for briar **pipe-making** and hand-crafted carpets; and special leather **sandals** – *les tropéziennes* – are made in St-Tropez. If you're seeking authenticity, then call in to *Les sandales tropéziennes* boutique (16 Rue Georges Clémenceau), which sells the leather and snakeskin items produced by the Rondini workshop, in operation since 1927. Keep an eye open too for *santons* – the charming clay figures dressed in traditional Provençal costume that were originally used as nativity characters.

Provençal **fabrics** are currently very much in vogue, largely due to market leaders such as *Souleïado* and *Les Olivades*. Their vivid modern interpretations of age-old designs are sold from their own boutiques in every major town but you will find similar fabrics, often made up into table linen, cushions and clothes, in souvenir shops and on market stalls at bargain prices.

## Food Products

Food is taken seriously all over France but the south has some very special treats. **Olive products** make lovely gifts: preserved olives (choose from tiny black niçoises olives, green olives from the Var, and purple olives from Nyons) and, of course, olive oil. One of the most famous olive oil producers is Alziari in Old Nice, where multi-hued olives are scooped out from great barrels and glorious golden oil is sold on draught from enormous casks. Look out for colourful bottles of oil flavoured with bunches of herbs and spices. *Tapenade* is a paste of black olives, anchovies and capers which is sold in little pots and is ideal for spreading on canapés. Dried **herbs** are another good buy, usually sold in hessian bags as *herbes de Provence*. **Preserved fruits** are a speciality of Nice; **crystallized violets** come from Tourettes-sur-Loup; Collobrières is famous for *marrons glacés* or **crystallized sweet chestnuts**. The abundance of fruit in the region is made into excellent jams. The quality of local home-produced honey is excellent too, especially when flavoured with various herbs. You will find specialist shops in most towns. On St-Honorat Island, don't miss the boutique at Lérins Abbey, where you can buy wine, *lavandin* (a hybrid lavender cultivated for its perfume essence) and honey, as well as the famous *Lérina* liqueur concocted from 45 aromatic plants.

## Perfumes of Provence

Flowers are essential to the Riviera scene, especially lavender which is sold distilled as lavender water or dried in pretty little sachets. Bunches of dried flowers are on sale everywhere and, as soap-making has been associated with Marseilles since the 16C, a wonderful selection of soaps is available, ranging from the olive-oil-based square blocks of traditional Marseilles soap (*savon de Marseille*) to charming hand-made soaps scented with floral essences. Perfumes produced from locally grown flowers and herbs are often sold from large glass containers with a small tap for filling individual bottles. For the best selection, visit the perfume town of Grasse.

# ENTERTAINMENT AND NIGHTLIFE

Since the opening of Monte-Carlo's casino in the middle of the 19C, **casinos** have become an essential part of the Riviera scene. The most renowned, besides the casino in *Monte-Carlo* (whose decor alone makes it worth a visit) are the *Grand Casino* in St-Raphaël

*An abundance of natural remedies on sale at Plan de la Tour.*

(Square de Gand), the *Casino Carlton Club* in Cannes (on the 7th floor of the prestigious luxury hotel, 58 La Croisette) and, in Nice, the *Casino Ruhl* on the Promenade des Anglais. Traditional games and slot machines enable anyone over the age of 21 (and wearing formal evening dress) to try their hand at Lady Luck...

A typical pleasant evening begins with an aperitif at a **pavement café** – ideal for tasting the ubiquitous *pastis* (not, however, obligatory!) accompanied by some nibbles (olives or grilled almonds)

whilst commenting on the last game of *pétanque* or the day's fishing. You'll find these everywhere, but some prestigious addresses merit being mentioned: at St-Paul-de-Vence, the *Café de la Place* (Pl du Général-de-Gaulle), still humming with conversations between artists and poets who were regular customers in days of old; at St-Tropez everyone, but everyone, has to be seen on the terrace of *Senequier* (Quai Jean-Jaurès); or to discuss one's latest yacht crossing at *Nano's* (Rue Sibille). And, in Monaco, there's no better observation post than the *Café de Paris* (Place du Casino)!

If you feel like prolonging your evening after dinner, you'll be spoilt for choice along the Riviera in resorts such as St-Tropez, Juan-les-Pins, Le Lavandou, Nice, Cannes or Monte-Carlo, with countless **discos** (open from 11pm till dawn). Of these, the most prestigious are, without doubt, *Les Caves du Roy* (Av du Maréchal-Foch, St-Tropez) and *Jimmy'z* (26 Av Princesse Grasse, Monaco).

Finally, why not end the evening sipping a drink in the sedate

Watersports are available at nearly all resorts in southern France.

atmosphere of the bar of a luxury hotel, often with a pianist tinkling away in the background? There's plenty of choice, from the *Amiral* in Cannes (73 La Croisette), the *Hôtel-palais Maeterlinck* (30 Bd Maurice Maeterlinck) and the sumptuous *Relais*, the bar of the hotel *Négresco* in Nice (37 Promenade des Anglais), or *La Terrasse*, the bar at Monaco's *Hermitage*, frequented by Onassis and La Callas in years past.

On the cultural side, **jazz** lovers are well served in July thanks to the Nice and Juan-les-Pins festivals. A number of **cinemas** show films in their original language (identified by the abbreviation v.o.) and the region offers a full programme of plays, concerts, ballets and operas (much esteemed in Marseilles, Toulon and Nice).

# SPORTS

## On the water's edge...

Watersports abound all along the coast, but **underwater diving** is worth special mention, in particular at Bendor (Centre Pradl); many clubs offer all-in prices with instruction. You can explore ancient sunken wrecks (thanks to the CIP Port-Fréjus, Aire de carénage, Port-Fréjus Est) or the undersea flora and fauna via the centres at Rayol-Canadel, Porquerolles and Port-Cros. The less adventurous can still explore underwater depths – and stay dry – aboard the **Seascope** glass-bottomed boats which leave from Le Lavandou and Port-Cros.

Above surface, you can try **sea kayaking** at Salins-d'Hyères, and **jet-skiing** at most of the major resorts. **Fun boarding** enthusiasts meet up on the beach at Almanarre, on the Giens peninsula, and **windsurfs** can be rented on most beaches. **Parascending** is also available at most beaches.

As for amateur yachtsmen, they have at their disposal a number of ports such as Bandol, Hyères (Port St-Pierre), La Londe (Miramar), Le Lavandou, St-Raphaël (Ste-Lucia), Cannes (Vieux Port) and Antibes (Port Vauban).

**Deep-sea fishing** enthusiasts can apply to Sanary, Cogolin Marina or Ste-Maxime to go on outings organised by the excursion boats (normally from 6-10am).

## ... or further inland

Discover the countryside astride a **mountain bike**. The Var tourism authorities publish a pamphlet listing 20 itineraries, and you will find the addresses of rental companies at the local tourist offices.

You can go **hiking** both along coastal paths and inland, where there are lots of long-distance footpaths. Alternatively, you can blaze a trail through the region on **horseback**... or astride a donkey in the Tinée Valley (*see* **Hiking** p.120).

The more adventurous can try **climbing** in the *niçois* mountains (e.g. Roquebrune-sur-Argens), while **winter sports** are available from December to April at Isola, Auron and Valberg.

## THE BASICS

### Before You Go

Visitors entering France should
have a full passport, valid to
cover the period in which they
will be travelling. Visitors from
EU countries need only a
national identity card. No visa
is required for members of EU
countries or US and Canadian
citizens, but visitors from New
Zealand and Australia may
require an entry visa. This can
be readily obtained from the
French Embassies and Con-
sulates in the home country.
No vaccinations are necessary.

### Getting There

Visitors to the South of France
have several travel options,
with driving from the Channel
ports or from elsewhere in
Europe being amongst the
most popular. One of the
fastest routes is by Le Shuttle,
which runs from Folkestone via
the Channel Tunnel to France
in 35 minutes; this service for
cars continues 24 hours a day
throughout the year.

Several ferry companies
carry cars and passengers
across the Channel, with the
quickest journeys being
between Dover/Calais, and
Folkestone/Boulogne. The
hovercraft is even faster,
crossing from Dover to Calais

in just 35 minutes. Brittany
Ferries offer crossings from
Portsmouth, Plymouth and
Poole directly to Brittany,
arriving at St Malo, Roscoff
and Cherbourg.

Once in France, the
autoroute runs directly from
Calais to the Riviera, but
although undoubtedly conve-
nient, this route has expensive
tolls and busy traffic throughout the months of July and
August. For those with time to
spare, the toll-free system of N

*A roof-top view across Bormes-les-Mimosas.*

and D roads (national and departmental) is well maintained and relatively quiet.

An efficient rail service connects the ports and Paris for foot passengers, or runs directly from London to Paris via Eurostar and the Channel Tunnel. From here there is the TGV fast train service to Avignon, Marseilles and Nice, and there are also high-speed trains to the south from many of the main European cities.

There are coach services throughout Europe, as well as between London and many towns in the South of France. If you plan to travel in the peak summer holiday period, be sure to book well in advance.

Two airports in the region of southern France – Nice and Marseilles – receive direct flights from the UK and many other countries.

# A-Z

## Accidents and Breakdowns

Fully comprehensive insurance is advisable for motorists in France, and motoring organizations recommend that you carry a green card, although this is no longer a legal requirement. A red warning triangle must be carried by cars towing a caravan or a trailer, in case of breakdown. While this is not compulsory for non-towing cars with hazard warning lights, it is strongly recommended.

On autoroutes there are orange emergency telephones every 2km (1.25 miles), and assistance is charged at a Government-fixed rate. Motorists can only call the police or the official breakdown service operating in that area, not their own breakdown company.

Check with your insurance company before leaving for France what you should do in case of an accident. Generally if an accident happens and nobody is hurt, a form *Constat à l'amiable* should be completed with full details. This must be signed by both parties, and sent off to the relevant insurers. If someone is injured in a road accident, telephone the Medical Emergency Service (*Samu*) ☎ 15, and the Police on ☎ 17.

## Accommodation

The region is ideal for holiday-makers seeking self-catering accommodation and good-quality campsites, as well as hotel and bed and breakfast rooms.

Staying in rural *gîtes* is a popular self-catering option. Details of over 2 000 properties can be obtained from: **Maison des Gîtes de France**, 59 Rue Saint Lazare, 75009 Paris; ☎ 01 49 70 75 75.

Bed and breakfast is available throughout France, and comes under the name *Café-Couette*, or *Chambres d'hôtes* – although these are not so popular in the South of France.

Campers and caravanners are extremely well catered for,

and there are sites both for those touring with their own equipment and for people wanting to hire on-site facilities. The French are passionate about camping, and their sites are generally of an excellent standard (*See also* **Camping**). For details of campsites in the South of France, consult the *Michelin Guide Camping Caravaning France*, or apply to: Fédération Française de Camping-Caravaning, 78 Rue de Rivoli, 75004 Paris; ☎ **01 42 72 84 08**.

Holders of an International Youth Hostel Federation card can apply for a list of French **youth hostels** to: La Ligue Française des Auberges de Jeunesse, 67 Rue Vergniaud, 75013 Paris; ☎ **01 44 16 78 78**; or at the Fédération Unie des Auberges de Jeunesse (FUAJ), 27 Rue Pajol, 75018 Paris ☎ **01 44 89 87 27**.

Information on all of the above accommodation can be obtained from the French Government Tourist Office in your own country (*see* **Tourist Information Offices**).
*For details of hotel accommodation, see p. 98.*

### Banks
Hours are: 9am-noon, 2-4pm but check locally as they can vary, weekdays, and banks are closed either on Mondays or Saturdays. They also close early on the day before a bank holiday. Banks exchange travellers' cheques, and most also have cash dispensers which accept international credit cards. A current passport is necessary when cashing cheques in a bank. Some banks, but not all, will change foreign money. *See also* **Money**

### Bicycles
These can be hired from main railway stations throughout the region, and may be returned to a different station at the end of the rental period. Tourist Offices provide lists of outlets that hire bikes, and further details of cycling on holiday are available from: Fédération Française de Cyclotourisme, 8 Rue Jean-Marie-Jégo, 75013 Paris; ☎ **01 44 16 88 88**.

Cyclists may also want to bring their own bicycles to France, and the ferries and many trains will carry them free.

### Camping
The French are very keen and very professional campers, and the country is well stocked with efficiently run sites offering a whole range of facilities. Some campsites offer fully equipped and permanently sited mobile

homes and family-sized tents, and details of these can usually be obtained through a travel agent or specialist company.

The *Michelin Guide Camping Caravaning France* lists a selection of sites, or contact **Fédération Française de Camping-Caravaning**, 78 rue de Rivoli, 75004 Paris ☎ **01 42 72 84 08**.

Touring sites are very well organized – you can choose from simple, basic sites in rural areas to large complexes with swimming pools, restaurants and entertainment. Those on or close to the Côte d'Azur can be expensive.

*The beach at Nice.*

## Car Hire

The South of France is well stocked with car hire agencies, and there are outlets at airports, air terminals and railway stations as well as in all large towns. Airlines and tour operators offer fly/drive arrangements, and car hire in conjunction with train travel is one of the services available from the French railway system (SNCF).

Weekly rates with unlimited mileage offer the best deal; these include collision damage waiver, personal accident insurance and local tax, and can be booked from any country. The minimum age limit is 18, but few international companies hire to drivers under 20-23.

Drivers must have held their full licence for at least a year, and an international driving licence is required for non-EU nationals. With the exception of Avis, there is maximum age limit of 60-65. Unless paying by credit card a substantial cash deposit is required, and full details of the different hire schemes can be obtained from Tourist Offices. Automatics are usually more expensive and should be booked in advance. *See also* **Accidents and Breakdowns**, and **Tourist Information Offices**

## Children

Even if the day is cloudy or the wind blowing, you can still burn on the south coast of France, so keep children – and yourself – well covered with sun cream and hats. The midday sun is especially fierce.

Restaurants in France, and especially in some of the less glamorous holiday resorts along the south coast, welcome children and are quite tolerant of less-than-perfect table manners. Those in the smarter towns and beach resorts may cater solely for the more sophisticated diner.

## Climate see p.94

## Climbing

For group outings accompanied by an instructor, contact the local offices of the **French Alpine Club** (Club Alpin français) in Toulon or Nice: 25 Rue Victor-Clappier, 83000 Toulon ☎ **04 94 46 26 63**; 14 Av Mirabeau, 06000 Nice ☎ **04 93 62 59 99**.

## Clothing

Comfortable casual clothing is ideal when holidaying in France. More formal dress may be expected at some restaurants and casinos on the Riviera, and here too you are judged by your appearance, so dress accord-ingly if you want to impress!

The people living in the countryside of southern France tend to be quite conservative, and whilst topless sunbathing is a fact of life by the sea, it is advisable to dress with more discretion in towns and rural areas.

The weather is generally extremely hot in the south during the summer months, but when the cold wind (*mistral*) blows down the Rhône Valley to the sea, warm clothes are definitely needed. Most French clothing measurements are standard throughout Europe but different from those in the UK and the USA. The following are examples:

**Dress Sizes**

| UK | 8 | 10 | 12 | 14 | 16 | 18 |
|---|---|---|---|---|---|---|
| France | 36 | 38 | 40 | 42 | 44 | 46 |
| US | 6 | 8 | 10 | 12 | 14 | 16 |

**Men's Suits**

| UK/US | 36 | 38 | 40 | 42 | 44 | 46 |
|---|---|---|---|---|---|---|
| France | 46 | 48 | 50 | 52 | 54 | 56 |

**Men's Shirts**

| UK/US | 14 | 14.5 | 15 | 15.5 | 16 | 16.5 | 17 |
|---|---|---|---|---|---|---|---|
| France | 36 | 37 | 38 | 39/40 | 41 | 42 | 43 |

**Men's Shoes**

| UK | 7 | 7.5 | 8.5 | 9.5 | 10.5 | 11 |
|---|---|---|---|---|---|---|
| France | 41 | 42 | 43 | 44 | 45 | 46 |
| US | 8 | 8.5 | 9.5 | 10.5 | 11.5 | 12 |

**Women's Shoes**

| UK | 4.5 | 5 | 5.5 | 6 | 6.5 | 7 |
|---|---|---|---|---|---|---|
| France | 37 | 38 | 38 | 39 | 39 | 40 |
| US | 6 | 6.5 | 7 | 7.5 | 8 | 8.5 |

### Complaints

Complaints about goods or services should ideally be made at the time. At a hotel or restaurant make your complaint in a calm manner to the manager. For more serious complaints, report your problem to the tourist office (*see* **Tourist Information Offices**) or, in the worst cases, to the police.

### Consulates

Embassies and consulates can be found at the following addresses:

**American Consulate**:
2 Rue St-Florentin, 75001 Paris;
☎ **01 43 12 22 22**.
Also at :
12 Boulevard Paul-Peytral, 13286 Marseilles;
☎ **04 91 54 92 00**.
31 Rue du Maréchal-Joffre, 06000 Nice
☎ **04 93 88 89 55**.
**Australian Embassy and Consulate**: 4 Rue Jean-Rey, 75016 Paris;
☎ **01 40 59 33 00**.
**British Consulate**:
16, Rue d'Anjou, 75008 Paris;
☎ **01 44 51 31 02**.
Also at:
24 Avenue du Prado, 13006 Marseilles;
☎ **04 91 15 72 10**.
**Canadian Embassy**:
35 Avenue Montaigne,

75008 Paris;
☎ **01 44 43 29 00**.
**Irish Embassy**:
4 Rue Rude, 75016 Paris;
☎ **01 44 17 67 00**.
**New Zealand Embassy**:
7 ter Rue Léonard-de-Vinci, 75016 Paris;
☎ **01 45 00 24 11**.

### Crime

Being the victim of theft can ruin a holiday, so take every precaution to prevent this happening to you. The best advice is to be aware at all times, carry as little money, and as few credit cards, as possible, and leave valuables in the hotel safe. Never leave your car unlocked. And don't leave any valuable items inside, since it can happen that cars are 'visited', particularly those near the beaches or in unguarded, isolated car parks.

If you have anything stolen, report it immediately to the nearest police station (*Commissariat de Police*), and collect a report so that you can make an insurance claim. If your passport is stolen, report it to the Consulate or Embassy at once. (*See also* **Lost Property**)

### Customs and Entry Regulations

There is no limit on the importation into France of tax-paid goods bought in an EU country provided they are for personal consumption, with the exception of alcohol and tobacco which have fixed limits governing them. Holiday-makers bringing a caravan into France for a period of less than six months are not governed by customs formalities.

### Disabled Visitors

The *Michelin Red Guide France* and *Michelin Camping Caravaning France* indicate which hotels and camp sites have facilities for disabled visitors. You can also get information on Minitel 3615 HANDITEL.

*Holidays and Travel Abroad: A Guide to Europe* is available from RADAR, 12 City Forum, 250 City Road, London EC1V 8AF ☎ 0171 250 3222 between 10am and 4pm. It contains advice and information about accommodation, transport, services, equipment and tour operators in Europe.

Travellers are strongly recommended to check their particular requirements first at the local Tourist Information Office, even when establishments advertise special facilities for the disabled.

### Driving

Drivers in France should carry a full national driving licence if they are EU citizens, or an international driving licence if they are not. Also required are insurance documents including a green card (no longer compulsory for EU members but strongly recommended), registration papers for the car, and a nationality sticker for the rear of the car.

Headlight beams should be adjusted for right-hand drive, and you should also have a spare set of light bulbs. Full or dipped headlights should be switched on at night or in poor visibility.

The minimum age for driving in France is 18. Front seat passengers must wear seatbelts, and back seat passengers must wear them where they are fitted. Children under ten travel in the rear of the car. Vehicles joining a road from the right have priority on all roads except those with a yellow diamond sign.

Those caught speeding or driving with a blood-alcohol level over the legal maximum (0.5g/litre) can be dealt with harshly, usually by on-the-spot fines. Driving is on the right-hand side of the road.

In some remote rural areas of Provence, petrol stations are in short supply, and they may be closed on Sundays. Speed limits are as follows:

*Built-up areas*: 50kph/31mph
*Dual carriageways and motorways without tolls*:
110kph/68mph (when raining, 100kph/62mph)
*Toll motorways*: 130kph/80mph (when raining, 110kph/68mph)
*Other roads:* 90kph/56mph (when raining, 80kph/50mph)
*Minimum speed limit on outside lane of motorways in good conditions:* 80kph/50mph.

**Tolls:** Most motorways are subject to a toll. You can pay in cash or by credit card.

For 24-hour road and route-planning information see Michelin on the Net under **Maps** or call *Interservice Route* ☎ 02 48 94 33 33. For information on all the French motorways ☎ 01 47 05 90 01, and for motorways in the South of France ☎ 08 36 69 36 36. If you have access to a Minitel dial **3615 ROUTE** (costs 1.29F/min). *See also* **Accidents and Breakdowns**

---

### Provençal Life and Traditions

**Boules:** the players can either play *à la longue* (take a three-pace run-up) or, most often, *à la pétanque* (keeping the feet in one spot). It's a question of *pointer*, in other words placing your ball as close as possible to the *but* or *cochonnet*. But watch out: the opposing team has some formidable *tireurs* whose *carreaux* can make mincemeat of all your hard work! The game continues in a series of *mènes* until a team reaches a score of 13 points.

**Cabanon:** a small house, often in wood, more often than not rather rickety, built by the sea where city-dwellers spend the weekend and summer holidays.

**Marché:** it's the place to meet, to catch up on the latest gossip, or simply revel in a multitude of sensations (aromas, colours, sounds)...and also where you'll get the best bargains. Don't miss the open-air markets, especially those inland. You can obtain your copy of the yearly calendar of arts and traditional craft markets from the Syndicat des Métiers d'Art du Var, BP 69, 83402 Hyères Cedex, ☎ 04 94 21 00 57.

**Pastis:** an aniseed-flavoured alcoholic drink, a real must at aperitif time! Served with lots of iced water, a refreshment with a southern accent.

**Santons:** dressed in old-fashioned Provençal village costumes, these dolls are essential onlookers in the nativity scenes portrayed in Provençal Christmas cribs. They can be found in December during the Santon Fairs (*foires aux santons*) in Marseilles (along the Canebière), Fréjus or Draguignan... or in July at Hyères and throughout the year at *santon* boutiques (Marcel Carbonnel, Rue Neuve Ste-Catherine, 13001 Marseilles, or in the Aubagne workshops).

*The harbour at St-Tropez.*

### Electric Current

The voltage in France – including on campsites – is usually 220V. Plugs and sockets vary greatly, though, and adaptors are generally required.

### Embassies *see* **Consulates**

### Emergencies

For an emergency requiring the Police, dial ☎ **17**; for the Fire Brigade ring ☎ **18**; and for an Ambulance (*Samu*) call ☎ **15**. The Operator's number is ☎ **13**, and Directory Enquiries is ☎ **12**. In some emergencies, the Consulate or Embassy might offer limited help. *See* **Consulates**

### Etiquette

As in most places in the world, it is considered polite and respectful to cover up decently in churches, museums and theatres.

The French are a more formal people than the British, shaking hands when they meet and addressing each other correctly by their title when they are not over familiar. Thus 'M'sieur' is the right way to address a police officer, and 'Bonjour Madame/Monsieur' should begin any conversation with a shopkeeper, post office clerk or hotel desk staff.

### Guidebooks *see* **Maps**

### Health

UK nationals should carry a Form E111 (forms available from post offices) which is produced by the Department of Health, and which entitles the holder to free urgent treatment for accident or illness in EU countries. The treatment will have to be paid for in the first instance, but can be reclaimed later. All foreign nationals are advised to take out comprehensive insurance cover, and to keep any bills, receipts and invoices to support any claim.

Lists of doctors can be obtained from hotels, chemists or police stations, and medical advice is also available at pharmacies (look out for the green cross). The latter are generally open from 2-7.30pm, Monday, 9am-7.30pm, Tuesday to Saturday, and those which are open late or on Sundays display notices on their doors, or on the doors of other pharmacies.

### Hiking

Among the long-distance footpaths (*sentiers de grande randonnée – GR*) for discovering the region, it's worth mentioning the GR 5 (Vésubie Gorges), 52 (via the Valley of the Marveilles through to Menton), 52A (Mercantour), 4 (Verdon Gorges), 9 (the Maures Mountain crossing) and 99 (from Toulon to the Verdon Gorges).

You can obtain ordinance survey maps (topoguides) in most libraries in the area or

from the French Hiking Federation (Fédération française de randonnée pédestre), CNSGR, 14 Rue Riquet, 75019 Paris ☎ 04 93 66 39 48.

A list of **riding stables** (*centres équestres*) is available from the Provence-Côte d'Azure League for Horse-Riding Tourism (*Ligue Provence-Côte d'Azur de tourisme équestre*), 19 Boulevard Victor Hugo, 06130 Grasse ☎ 04 93 42 62 98; the Estérel Centre for Horse-Riding Tourism (*Centre de tourisme équestre de l'Estérel*), Domaine du Grenouillet, Agay, 83700 St-Raphaël ☎ 04 94 82 75 28; or the *Comité départemental d'équitation de randonnée des Alpes-Maritimes*, Mas de la Jumenterie, Route de St-Cézaire, 06460 St-Vallier-de-Thiey ☎ 04 93 42 62 98.

For exploring the Tinée Valley, astride a donkey, contact Itinérance, Hameau de Villeplane, 06470 Guillaumes ☎ 04 93 05 56 01.

### Language

The Provençal language is still taught as an option in schools although French is the spoken language of the region. Your efforts to speak French will be much appreciated, and even a few simple words and expressions are often warmly received. The table above has a

Good morning  Bonjour
Goodbye  Au revoir
Yes/no  Oui/non
Please/thank you  S'il vous plaît/merci
Sorry  Pardon
Do you speak English?  Parlez-vous anglais?
I want to buy  Je voudrais acheter
How much is it?  Quel est le prix?
The bill, please  L'addition, s'il vous plaît
I'd like a booklet of tickets  Je voudrais un carnet de tickets
Is service included?  Le service est-il compris?
Black espresso  Un café *or* un express
White coffee  Un café au lait/crème
Fresh lemon/orange juice  Un citron pressé/une orange pressée
A bottled beer  Une bouteille de bière
A draught beer  Une bière pression

few words and phrases to help you make the most of your stay.

**Lost Property**

Airports and major railway stations have their own lost property offices (*Objets trouvés*), but if something goes missing in your hotel, check with the front desk and hotel security. Report all lost or stolen items to the police, and always make sure to get a report to substantiate any insurance claims when you get home.

Should you lose any travel documents, contact the police, and in the event of a passport going missing inform your Embassy or Consulate immediately (*see* **Consulates**). Lost or stolen travellers' cheques and credit cards should be reported immediately to the issuing company with a list of numbers, and the police should also be informed.

**Maps**

The *Michelin Road Map Provence-Côte d'Azur* (**No.245**) and the more detailed maps **Nos. 114** and **115** will provide you with clear information on towns, villages and main routes. The *Michelin Green Guide French Riviera* contains town plans for the larger towns and cities and detailed itineraries of the region. In addition, it has full details of the main sights and attractions within the region.

## Monaco – Before You Go

An independent state, there are certain things you should be aware of before visiting the principality of Monaco. The telephone code is **00-377**.

Once there, you can use your French money, but you may be given change in Monacan currency, which has no value elsewhere (though it is sometimes accepted in the Alpes-Maritimes). So spend any change before you leave...why not buy local stamps, which are obligatory for any mail posted within the Principality.

## Money

The French unit of currency is the franc, which is divided into 100 centimes. Bank notes are issued in denominations of 500F, 200F, 100F, 50F and 20F, while coins come in 20F, 10F, 5F, 2F, 1F and 50c (all silver apart from the 20F and 10F coins which have a bronze border and the older bronze-coloured 10F coin), and the bronze-coloured 20c, 10c and 5c coins.

There are no restrictions on the amount of currency visitors can take into France, but the safest way to carry large amounts of money is in travellers' cheques, which are widely accepted and exchanged.

Bureaux de change are found at airports, terminals and larger railway stations, and at banks (see also **Banks**).

Exchange rates vary, so it pays to shop around. American Express, Carte Bleue (Visa/Barclaycard), Diners Club and Eurocard (Mastercard/Access) are widely accepted. Always check the total which appears on the receipt, and note that in France there is a comma between francs and centimes.

Lost or stolen travellers' cheques and credit cards should be reported immediately to the issuing company with a list of numbers, and the police should also be informed.

**Euro:** 1999 saw the launch of the European Single Currency: the Euro. In France, as well as in ten other countries in the European Union, prices are today displayed in the local currency and in Euros. However, as Euro notes and coins will not be available until 2002, payment in Euros is currently only possible by bank or credit cards (the fixed rate between the Euro and the Franc is 1Euro = 6.55957F).

## Newspapers

In the main towns and cities of southern France, English-language newspapers are easily obtainable. French daily newspapers include *Le Monde*, and *Le Figaro*, and regional papers *Nice Matin*, *La Marseillaise*, *Le Provençal* and *Le Méridional*.

## Opening Hours

Chemists are generally open 2-7.30pm Monday, 9am-7.30pm Tuesday to Saturday, and some open later and on Sundays. Gendarmeries have their addresses, and a list of late-night or 24-hour openings can be found on all pharmacy doors. **Museums and monuments** are generally open from 10am-noon and 2-5.30pm. Many stay open later in summer. National museums and art galleries are closed on Tuesdays, whereas municipal museums are closed on Mondays. *See also* **Shopping** p.104, **Banks** and **Post Offices**

## Police

In towns and cities, French police wear a dark blue uniform and a flat cap, and are known as the *Police*, while in country areas and small towns they are *Gendarmes*, and wear blue trousers, dark blue jackets and a white belt. The police are addressed as 'M'sieur', and in emergencies can be contacted on ☎ 17. Police can impose and collect on-the-spot fines for drivers who violate traffic regulations.

## Post Offices

Post offices are open Monday to Friday, 8am-7pm (although smaller ones may be closed at lunch-time) and Saturday 8am-noon. Some are also open at other times but only offer a limited service. Stamps are also available from newsagents and tobacconists, and some hotels.

Air mail letters and post cards to the UK cost 3F; aerogrammme to the USA 5F, letter or postcard to the USA 4.40F, and a letter (20g) to Australia and New Zealand 5.20F. Poste restante mail should be sent to the person at Poste Restante, Poste Centrale, postal code of *département* followed by town name, France, and a passport should be taken along as proof of identity when collecting mail. Note that French stamps are not valid on mail sent from Monaco.

## Public Holidays

New Year's Day: 1 January
Easter Sunday/Monday (*Pâques*)
May Day: 1 May
VE Day: 8 May
Ascension Day: 40 days after
    Easter
Whitsun (*Pentecôte*): 7th Sunday
    and Monday after Easter
Bastille Day: 14 July
Assumption Day: 15 August
All Saints' Day (*Toussaint*):
    1 November

Remembrance Day:
11 November
Christmas Day: 25 December

## Religion

France is largely a Roman Catholic country, and every town has a Catholic church. The other major religions are often represented in larger towns and cities, with synagogues in Nice and Marseilles. For particular details of services, ask at any tourist information office.

## Smoking

Cigarettes and pipe tobacco are on sale at *Tabacs*, the licensed tobacconists displaying red carrot-shaped signs, and also drugstores and some restaurants and bars. New laws prohibit smoking in any public building. Bars and restaurants should all have a no-smoking zone.

## Telephones

Many public telephones take phonecards (*télécartes*) which can be bought from post offices, tobacconists, newsagents, and at outlets advertized on telephone booths.

French telephone numbers have 10 digits. Paris and Paris region numbers begin with **01**, those in the North-West of France with **02**, in the North-East with **03**, in the South-East with **04**, and in the South-West

with **05**.

Cheap rate with up to 65 per cent extra time is from 9pm – 8am Monday to Friday, and weekends from noon on Saturdays. Calls can be received at phone boxes with the blue bell sign. Numbers beginning with **0 800** are free of charge.

To call abroad from France, first dial **00** and wait for the continuous tone, then dial **44** plus STD code (minus first 0) followed by the number for the UK, **61** for Australia, **1** for Canada and the USA, **64** for New Zealand and **353** for Eire.

**Emergency numbers:** Fire ☎ **18**; Police ☎ **17**; Ambulance (*Samu*) ☎ **15**; Operator ☎ **13**; Directory Enquiries ☎ **12**. For international enquiries dial **00 33 12** plus the country code.

## Time Difference

French standard time is GMT plus one hour. French summer time begins on the last Sunday in March at 2am when the clocks go forward an hour (the same day as British Summer Time), and ends on the last Sunday in September at 3am, when the clocks go back (one month before BST ends).

## Tipping

In France, a 15 per cent service charge is usually included at hotels and restaurants; if you pay by cash it is polite to leave small change for the waiter.

Public lavatory attendants with saucers may be happy with a few coins, but sometimes the price is displayed and is not negotiable. Tipping of 15 per cent is normal for taxi drivers, but not obligatory. A loose guide for tipping is: Hotel porter, per bag 5F; Hotel maid, per week 50-100F; Lavatory attendant 2F; Tour guide 10F.

### Tourist Information Offices

The French Government Tourist Office is an excellent first source of information for everything you will need to know during your stay.

**OVERSEAS OFFICES:**
**Australia**: BNP Building, 12th Floor, 12 Castlereagh Street, Sydney, NSW 2000;
☎ 612 231 5244.
**Canada**: 1981 Avenue McGill College, Suite 490, Montreal, Quebec H3A 2W9;
☎ 514 288 4264.
**Ireland**: 35 Lower Abbey Street, Dublin 1; ☎ 1 703 4046.
**UK**: Maison de la France, 178 Piccadilly, London W1V 0AL;
☎ 0891 244123
**USA: France On Call Hotline**
☎ 900 990 0040 ($.50 per min) for information on hotels, restaurants and transportation; East Coast – 444 Madison

Avenue, New York, NY 10020-10022; ☎ 212 838 7800.
Mid West – 676 North Michigan Avenue, Suite 3360, Chigago, IL 60611;
☎ 312 751 7800.
West Coast – 9454 Wilshire Boulevard, Suite 715 Beverley Hills, CA 90212;
☎ 310 271 2693.

**LOCAL TOURIST OFFICES:**
Comité Régional de Tourisme, **Provence-Alpes-Côte d'Azur**, 14 Rue Sainte Barbe, 13241 Marseilles Cedex 01;
☎ 04 91 39 38 00.
**Alpes-de-Haute Provence**, Boulevard Victor-Hugo, BP 170, 04005 Digne Cedex;
☎ 04 92 31 57 29.
**Riviera-Côte d'Azur**, 55 Promendade des Anglais, BP 602, 06011 Nice Cedex 1;
☎ 04 93 37 78 78.
**Bouches-du-Rhône**, 13 Rue Roux de Brignoles, 13006 Marseilles;
☎ 04 91 13 84 13.
**Comité départemental du Tourisme du Var**, 1 Bd Foch, BP 99, 83003, Draguignan Cedex;
☎ 04 94 50 55 60.
**Vaucluse**, Place Campana, La Balance, BP 147, 84008 Avignon;
☎ 04 90 80 47 00.
**Principauté de Monaco** 2A, Boulevard des Moulins

98000 Monaco
☎ **00 377 93 50 60 88**.

As well as local information, Tourist information centres (*Offices de tourisme*) also provide accommodation and restaurant lisitngs. Tourist information is also available from town halls (*mairie*).

## Transport

The French railway system (SNCF) operates an extensive network throughout France, including many high-speed trains (TGV) and motorail services. There is a railway line up the Durance Valley into the Alps, a narrow gauge railway from Nice to Digne, and a single-track mountain railway from Nice into Italy.

There are many different types of reduced-price tickets – enquire at the French Tourist Office in your own country for details before travelling, or at the tourist information centres or SNCF offices in France.

The SNCF also run bus services between railway stations and the surrounding areas. Most larger towns have a bus service, and many country areas have a reasonable, if infrequent, service.

There are taxi ranks – *tête de station* – outside railway stations and in town centres. Taxis can also be hailed in the street in large cities, or you can order

one by telephone (look up *Taxi* in the phone book).

The best way to explore the region is by car, as many places are otherwise inaccessible.

## TV and Radio

Almost all TV programmes are in French, but English radio programmes are broadcast in the summer, and BBC stations can be picked up easily on short or medium-wave radios. The English-language Radio Riviera and Monte-Carlo TV can be picked up along the Côte d'Azur.

## Water

Water served in hotels and restaurants is perfectly safe to drink, as is tap water unless labelled '*eau non potable*' (not drinking water).

## Weather Forecasts

General weather information:
☎ **08 36 68 00 00**
**Recorded reports**
For Alpes-Maritimes:
☎ **08 36 68 02 06**
For the Var:
☎ **08 36 68 02 83**
**Conditions at sea**
For Alpes-Maritimes:
☎ **08 36 65 08 06**
For the Var:
☎ **08 36 65 08 83**
5-day forecasts 08 36 65 08 08

# INDEX

This index includes entries in both English (where used in the guide) and in French (italics).

# INDEX